Essential Tenerife

by Andrew Sanger

Andrew Sanger is a well-established travel journalist who has contributed to a wide range of popular magazines and most British newspapers. He is the author of many travel guides, including *AA Explorer Israel* and *AA Essential Lanzarote & Fuerteventura.*

Above: *the view from Mirador de la Garanora framed by palm fronds*

AA Publishing

Above: *a splendid resident of the Loro Parque at Puerto de la Cruz*

Front cover: *Playa de las Teresitas; tiled bench at Santa Cruz; farmer in traditional costume at a fiesta*
Back cover: *grape harvest*

Written by Andrew Sanger

First published 2000
Reprinted Feb and Aug 2000; Feb and Sep 2001; Feb 2002.

Published by AA Publishing, a trading name of Automobile Association Developments Limited, whose registered office is Millstream, Maidenhead Road, Windsor SL4 5GD. Registered number 1878835.

A CIP catalogue record for this book is available from the British Library.
ISBN 0 7495 2213 5

The contents of this publication are believed correct at the time of printing. Nevertheless, the publishers cannot be held responsible for any errors or omissions or for changes in the details given in this guide or for the consequences of any reliance on the information provided by the same. Assessments of attractions, hotels, restaurants and so forth are based upon the author's own experience and, therefore, descriptions given in this guide necessarily contain an element of subjective opinion which may not reflect the publisher's opinion or dictate a reader's own experience on another occasion.

We have tried to ensure accuracy in this guide, but things do change and we would be grateful if readers would advise us of any inaccuracies they may encounter.

Colour separation: Chroma Graphics (Overseas) Pte Ltd, Singapore
Printed and bound in Italy by Printer Trento Srl

Contents

About this Book

KEY TO SYMBOLS

- map reference to the maps found in the What to See section
- address or location
- telephone number
- opening times
- restaurant or café on premises or near by
- nearest underground train station
- nearest bus/tram route
- nearest overground train station
- ferry crossings and boat excursions
- travel by air
- tourist information
- facilities for visitors with disabilities
- admission charge
- other places of interest near by
- other practical information
- ➤ indicates the page where you will find a fuller description

Essential *Tenerife* is divided into five sections to cover the most important aspects of your visit to Tenerife.

Viewing Tenerife pages 5–14
An introduction to Tenerife by the author.
Tenerife's Features
Essence of Tenerife
The Shaping of Tenerife
Peace and Quiet
Tenerife's Famous

Top Ten pages 15–26
The author's choice of the Top Ten places to see in Tenerife, each with practical information.

What to See pages 27–90
The three main areas of Tenerife, plus La Gomera, each with a brief introduction and an alphabetical listing of the main attractions.
Practical information
Snippets of 'Did you know…' information
4 suggested walks
4 suggested tours
2 features

Where To... pages 91–116
Detailed listings of the best places to eat, stay, shop, take the children and be entertained.

Practical Matters pages 117–24
A highly visual section containing essential travel information.

Maps
All map references are to the individual maps found in the What to See section of this guide.

For example, Puerto de la Cruz has the reference 28C4 – indicating the page on which the map is located and the grid square in which the town is to be found. A list of the maps that have been used in this travel guide can be found in the index.

Prices
Where appropriate, an indication of the cost of an establishment is given by **£** signs:
£££ denotes higher prices, **££** denotes average prices, while **£** denotes lower charges.

Star Ratings
Most of the places described in this book have been given a separate rating:

✪✪✪	Do not miss
✪✪	Highly recommended
✪	Worth seeing

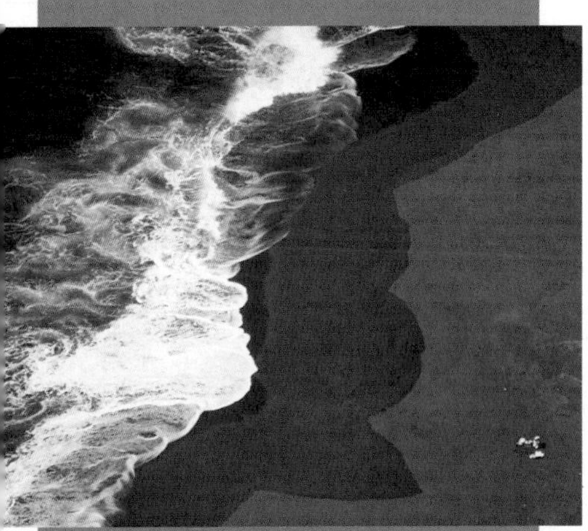

Viewing Tenerife

Above: *Looking down on the beach from Mirador de la Garanora*
Right: *Spectators in traditional dress at the Fiesta Romera, Santa Cruz*

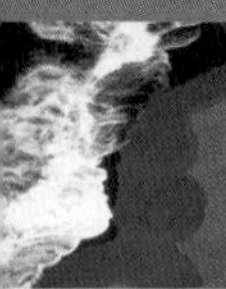

Andrew Sanger's Tenerife

The Canaries
There are 13 islands all together in the volcanic Canaries archipelago, seven of them populated (the other six are tiny). Home to the native Guanches from the 3rd millennium BC, the Canary Islands were claimed by the Spanish in the 15th century. Though distant from the mainland, they remain administratively part of Spain.

Above: *forest near Vilaflor, which means the 'Flower Town'*

A layer of tourism clings to the surface of Tenerife. That's not all bad – it's following in a 100-year-old tradition, and gives the island an income. Most visitors stay in sun-baked southern parts of the island where locals have never lived, and usually remain there throughout their visit. So tourism, while never harmless, does surprisingly little damage to Tenerife even though it's Europe's most popular winter sun destination.

For me, the challenge is to get beneath that surface. Peel back the layer of tourism and you'll discover that Tenerife is not just a holiday isle: it's colonial Spain. Here is a Spain we don't see much on the mainland: a reminder of the *conquistadores*, an immediate sense of Spain's enterprise, power and wealth centuries ago. The Canaries feel close to the colonies in Latin America, where so many *Tinerfeños* went to live.

Here as well is the Spain of today. Take a side turn, explore the villages, get into the hills, or the backstreets of Santa Cruz or La Laguna, and holiday land seems to vanish like morning mist. Here are the real bars and *restaurantes*, the plazas and glazed tiles and the sounds and the people of the Iberian peninsula.

However, that too can be peeled back to reveal another level. Leave the villages and backstreets behind, walk alone in the balmy, luxuriant hills, or in the desolate Cañadas. The Guanches are long gone, but there's an air of mystery about Tenerife that these native islanders bequeathed. Through them, I see that Tenerife belongs neither to the tourists nor to the Spanish, but to the Atlantic, to Africa, and to the snow-capped volcano which gave the island its Guanche name.

Tenerife's Features

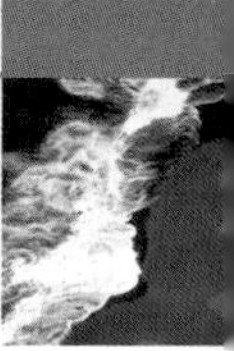

Position

Tenerife lies in the western half of the Canary Islands archipelago, just under 500km north of the Tropic of Cancer and only about 300km from the coast of the Western Sahara, in Africa. La Gomera lies 32km from Tenerife's southwestern shore.

Size

The largest of the Canary Islands, Tenerife (pronounced *Ten-air-reef-eh* in Spanish) covers 2,057sq km. It's 130km across at its widest point, and 90km from north to south. By contrast, La Gomera, its next-door neighbour, is almost the smallest of the Canaries, just 23km by 25km.

A Long Way from Spain

Though Spanish, Tenerife is much closer to the Sahara than to Spain – only around 300km from the coast of Africa, the island lies 1,120km from Spain. Until the start of air travel in the 1950s, Tenerife was remote and little visited.

A huge bronze sculpture of a theatrical mask dominates the steps of the Teatro Guimera in Santa Cruz

People

Only 650,000 people live on Tenerife, and about 20,000 on La Gomera. They're outnumbered by four million tourists annually.

Climate

Like the other Canaries, Tenerife and La Gomera are strongly influenced by the prevailing trade winds, bringing moist air or rain – but only to the north. The south of Tenerife and La Gomera remain practically rain-free all year round, though there can be winter cloud. Any rain that does fall normally comes between October and February. Average daytime temperatures remain about 22ºC all year round. Both islands can be windy, especially on the west.

Language

Spanish is the language of the Canary Islands, with a few indigenous words still in use. English is widely spoken (especially at tourist resorts) though often not very well.

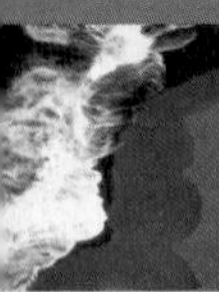

Essence of Tenerife

Tenerife is like two places in one. In the north, it's Spanish and lived-in, with authentic working towns and villages. In the south, it's a basking holiday land of vibrant entertainment, resorts and hotels, devoted to giving millions of visitors a fortnight of fun. While the north has an almost tropical, productive lushness, the south is rainless and dry.

The combination of the two gives Tenerife tremendous appeal. For many visitors, nothing can tear them away from days in the sun and nights on the town. For others, it's a delight to explore the 'real' Tenerife, getting to know this beautiful volcanic land and its people. And some, of course, enjoy both sides of Tenerife.

Above: *the founder of the Museo Municipal de Bellas Artes, Santa Cruz*

Below: *children on a float at the Fiesta Romera*

THE 10 ESSENTIALS

If you only have a short time to visit Tenerife, or would like to get a really complete picture of the island, here are the essentials:

- **Go up El Teide** The high point of Tenerife, a snow-capped dormant volcano worshipped by the Guanches, the original inhabitants of the island. From here you can see almost the whole of the Canary Islands (➤ 18).
- **Experience Playa de las Américas** Leave the real world behind and enter the package holiday dreamland, in a purpose-built town of artificial beaches, all-night discos, English pubs and restaurants that proudly boast 'No Spanish Food Served Here!' (➤ 74–5).

- **Go bananas** Eat Tenerife bananas, have them flambéd for dessert, drink banana liqueur, buy souvenirs made of banana leaves and visit Bananera el Guanche (➤ 55) – all because bananas are an important crop here.
- **Eat a Canarian stew** Try *potaje, rancho canario* or *puchero* – vegetables and meat simmered to a savoury perfection. With bread, locals consider it a complete meal.
- **Get spicy** You must try the pleasantly spicy local sauce called *mojo*. Served with fish or *papas arrugadas* (wrinkly potatoes), it's the most Canarian thing on the menu.
- **Drink a local wine** One of the first big successes for colonial Tenerife was the development of drinkable wines to rival those in mainland Spain. The island's wines have remained important ever since. La Gomera, too, has good local wines.
- **Get out of the resorts** Walk, drive or cycle, but one way or another see the Tenerife most tourists miss.
- **Watch a whale** Join one of the boat excursions to see the whales and dolphins which live just off southern Tenerife and La Gomera (➤ 112).
- **Have fun at a fiesta** It's an unusual fortnight in the Tenerife calendar that doesn't have at least one fiesta. Ask the tourist office what's on next.
- **Go to another island** Take the ferry to La Gomera, and find the truly unspoiled Canaries. If you're staying on La Gomera, take the boat trip over just to visit El Teide.

Above: *a wine cellar sign in Icod de los Vinos, a town justly famed for its wines*

Above: *sand was brought from the Sahara to create Playa de las Teresitas*

Inset: *a disco at Playa de las Américas*

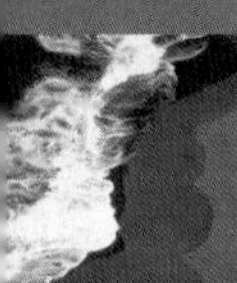

The Shaping of Tenerife

2–20 million years ago
Huge volcanic eruptions create the Canary Islands, starting with the most easterly and heading west. Tenerife appears 10 million years ago.

2500–2000 BC
Tenerife is peopled by the Guanches, believed to have been Berbers, the nomadic pastoralists of North Africa, strongly influenced by the civilisation and culture of ancient Egypt. When the first Europeans arrive much later, the Guanches still mummify their dead and speak a language recognisably derived from that of the Berbers.

12th–1st century BC
Phoenician and other sailors visit the Canary Islands. From antiquity the archipelago is known as The Fortunate Isles.

***c* AD 1**
On behalf of the Romans, Juba II of Mauretania sends an expedition to explore the Fortunate Isles. Some of the islands are then named, one being called Canaria for its wild dogs (from the Latin *canis*, dog); the islands take the name Canaries.

***c* 1000**
Arab raiders pay a first visit, take a few Guanche slaves and call the islands Kaledat.

Left: *statues of Guanche chieftains line the sea wall at Candelaria*

1312
Genoese sailor Lancelotto Malocello visits Fuerteventura and Lanzarote (which is a corruption of his name), the first European colonist in the Canaries.

1350–1450
Assorted raiders and slavers pause at the Canaries for the purpose of capturing slaves.

1402
Two Norman adventurers, Gadifer de la Salle and Jean de Béthencourt, set out to conquer the Canaries. Although only taking Lanzarote, they claim all the islands for the king of Spain, who financed their trip.

Early 1400s
On more easterly islands, Norman and Spanish settlers enslave the Guanche natives and build European-style farming villages, but Tenerife remains unconquered.

1494–5
A determined and ruthless Spanish colonist, Alonso Fernández de Lugo, financed by Genoese merchants and equipped with 1,000 mercenaries, attacks Tenerife. Most of his men are ambushed and killed by the Guanches. The next year, de Lugo

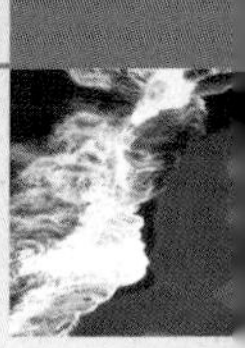

returns with more men and conquers the island, killing thousands of Guanches. Plots of land handed out to investors in his expedition are developed as sugar plantations. Portuguese and Spanish labourers are shipped in to work the new farms.

16th–17th centuries
Destructive French, English, Dutch and Arab pirates and privateers harass Tenerife, attracted by the laden merchant ships coming from the New World, pausing at Santa Cruz. Tenerife's various fortifications date from this period.

18th century
Grapes are planted and soon wine is an important product. Tenerife becomes a civilised and cultured hideaway for European nobility and wealthy traders.

1797
Horatio Nelson launches an attack on Santa Cruz. The objectives: to take the town, to seize the gold-laden ship *El Príncipe d'Asturias* and to show the French who is supreme on the high seas. In the only failure of his career, Nelson retreats having lost his right arm after being injured by a cannonball.

19th century
The wine trade collapses, but is replaced first by the cultivation of cochineal beetles (for their dye), which are raised on plantations of cacti, and then by bananas, soon the main crop. The banana boats also carry passengers, and the island becomes a fashionable resort for wealthy British scholars, writers and artists. One of the first guidebooks is written – *Tenerife and its six satellites* (by Olivia Stone, 1887).

1914–18
The Great War causes massive emigration.

1936
General Franco, *Comandante-Generale* of the Canary Islands, is based on Tenerife as he plans a right-wing coup to take over Spain. On 18 July, the Spanish Civil War (1936–9) starts with the virtually unopposed Nationalist takeover of Tenerife. A week later Franco has control of all the Canaries. He leaves Tenerife to take command of his rebel army on the mainland.

Early 1960s
Package tourism to the Canaries begins. Tenerife is immediately successful, with the transformation of Puerto de la Cruz into the island's first resort.

1978
International airport Reina Sofía opens on the south coast. Playa de las Américas begins to be developed.

Late 1980s
Almost all Canary bananas now go to Spain.

1980–90s
Tourism reaches huge proportions and becomes the island's main source of income.

2000
Plans are made to take tourism up-market and reduce visitor numbers.

Below: *the international airport at Reina Sofía*

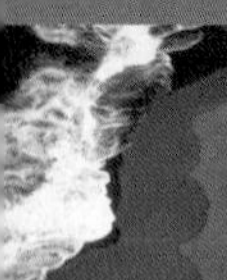

Peace & Quiet

Despite Tenerife's clamour and crowds, much of the island remains tranquil – it is easy to escape from the excesses of tourism. Remember too that most tourists wake up late: even popular spots enjoy relative peace in the mornings.

The desert-like south possesses a magical quality of stillness and silence. In the central uplands, pine-covered slopes reach into an awesome rocky terrain carved by the volcanic power of El Teide. The lush green northern hills, draped year-round with wild blossom, are a delight that few visitors discover. Almost anywhere off the beaten track, the country is coloured with masses of nasturtiums and hibiscus, marigolds and carnations, geraniums and hanging bougainvillea.

Clearly marked paths lead walkers through the stunning mountainous countryside around Chinamada

Quiet country paths are a feature of the island, and make a pleasant break for an interesting stroll, getting to know Tenerife's character and landscapes. Keen ramblers could spend a fortnight on the island and barely see another foreigner, taking more isolated trails to climb and explore the interior.

You don't need to be a strong walker to discover all this. Car drivers will soon find picnic spots away from the main roads. ICONA, Spain's environmental protection organisation, has created beautifully located picnic places all over the island. Some 2,000 species of plantlife flourish

Wildflowers in the Teide National Park

Trees in the Valle de la Oratava rising above a layer of cloud

here, with much of the flauna and flora being unique to the island. It's worth adding that Tenerife is mercifully free of troublesome insects, and there are no poisonous snakes.

On the dry southern shores, cacti and palms thrive, while along the northern and western coasts, semi-tropical varieties abound. Here are woods of mimosa, jacaranda and rubber trees, wild roses and poinsettia, and, of course, those Tenerife marvels, the mighty Dragon Tree (*Dracaena draco*) and the gentle bird-of-paradise flower (strelitzia).

The centre of Tenerife, in and around the Teide National Park, contrasts the abundant greenery of Orotava with the drama of Las Cañadas and the intriguing rare plants of the Teide. The most striking is the giant bugloss (*Echium wildpretii*) with amazing erect red flower clusters as much as two metres long. High on the slopes, the Teide violet (*Viola cheiranthifolia*) may be found – treat it carefully, it's very rare and lives only here. The Teide daisy and Teide broom, too, are endemic. The mountainsides are covered with pine and palm. On upper slopes, pockets survive of the islands' once extensive *Laurasilva*, or forests of Canary laurel (*Larus canariensis*).

Take a boat across to La Gomera for a more perfect peace. Get well away from San Sebastián, where the ferry disembarks, heading west into the hinterland of this undeveloped Canary Island, deeply scored with *barrancos* (gorges). Its central mountain region is thickly covered with Canary laurel forest, and on the coasts it is still possible to find sun, sea – and solitude.

Spectacular flowering cacti thrive on Tenerife

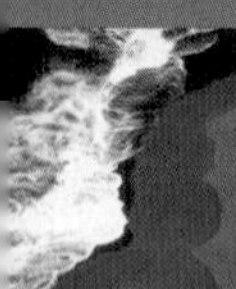

Famous of Tenerife & La Gomera

The Franco Connection
General Francisco Franco, the dictator whose police state ruled Spain with an iron hand from 1939 to 1975, launched his coup from Tenerife, where he lived as *Comandante-Generale* for four months in 1936. For old times' sake he took a holiday on the island in 1953 .

Tomás de Iriarte

The small population of the island of Tenerife, largely illiterate until the 1970s, has produced few famous sons. One of the most important was 18th-century satirical writer and translator Tomás de Iriarte (1750–91), whose works were highly successful on the mainland. They included a collection of fables, *Fábulas Literarias*, and many translations of the Roman poet and satirist Horace.

Simon Bolívar

The South American revolutionary Simon Bolívar perhaps qualifies as a famous grandson. Bolívar, who struggled successfully at the head of the liberation movement to free Latin America from Spanish rule, was the grandchild of poor emigrants who left Tenerife looking for a better life in the Americas. A statue of the revolutionary stands at Garachico, their home town. That connection explains Simon Bolívar's references to the Canaries – along with the South America states – as Spanish colonies yearning for freedom.

Nelson's mission was to capture Spanish treasure ships rumoured to be in the Canaries

Horatio Nelson

Admiral Horatio Nelson, like some modern tourists, didn't so much visit Tenerife as invade it. His attack on Santa Cruz in 1797 proved to be the only failure of his illustrious career in the service of the British crown. Newly promoted to rear admiral, he was sent to sieze a Spanish ship laden with treasure, but the forces he was provided with were insufficient for the task. Nelson lost his right arm in the conflict; he stayed on the island just long enough for himself and his men to be treated by local doctors.

Christopher Columbus

By far the most famous person ever associated with the island of La Gomera was Christopher Columbus, the explorer and entrepreneur who stayed there before setting out to discover whether a westward trade route existed to the Indies. His first visit in 1492 was for the purpose of making final checks and supplies before the pioneering Atlantic crossing. Becoming friendly with the island's countess Beatriz de Bombadilla, he visited La Gomera twice more before his Atlantic voyages.

Top Ten

Above: *Garachico, from San Juan del Repard*
Right: *the restored façade of the Casa de los Balcones, Orotava*

1

Casa de los Balcones, La Orotava

29D4

3 Calle San Francisco, La Orotava

Mon–Fri 9–1.30, 4–7.30, Sat 9–1.30

Many unpretentious restaurants and bars, for example Bar Parada (£) in Plaza de la Constitución

Nos 345 and 350 (Puerto de la Cruz–La Orotava) every 20–30 mins and No 348 same route once daily

1 Plaza General Franco
922 33 00 50

None

Cheap

La Orotava (► 65)

The Casa is famous for the intricately carved balconies in its courtyard

The most famous sight in the sedate, balconied Spanish colonial hilltown of La Orotava is an intriguing 17th-century mansion

Pretty potted geraniums decorate the balconies looking over Calle San Francisco. It's not the balconies on the outside, though, that give the house its name: enter the impressive front doors and you will find the exquisitely carved wooden balconies of the interior courtyard. Here abundant refreshing greenery, earthenware pots and an old wine press give a cool, elegant air. The building's history is told in the museum upstairs: originally two separate houses, the Casa was first built in 1632 as homes for prosperous colonists.

Downstairs in the busy souvenir and craft shop, a major stop-off point for coach tours, an additional attraction is local craftspeople demonstrating how to roll a cigar, weave a basket, or paint sand in readiness for the big Corpus Christi celebrations. This unusual shop sells, in addition to popular cheap souvenirs, a wide range of high-quality items such as Spanish and Canarian lace and linen, and traditional handcrafted Canarian embroideries. Some small items – such as handkerchiefs – give an opportunity to buy good quality local goods at affordable prices.

Some of the embroideries are made on the premises, as the Casa de los Balcones also serves as a highly regarded school for embroidery. For over 50 years the school has been training small numbers of pupils in the traditional methods and designs of Canarian embroidery, which would perhaps have disappeared altogether if not for its efforts.

2
Drago Milenario

The drago *or dragon tree is a species peculiar to the Canaries, and this amazing, ancient example has become the symbol of Tenerife.*

Icod de los Vinos is home to the legendary Dragon Tree

Just how old is this extraordinary tree? The name means 'Thousand Year Drago' – and many brochure writers pile on the years to absurd figures, like two or even three thousand years. In reality, this majestic specimen, the oldest known, probably dates back about 600 years.

More remarkable perhaps is that the species itself – *Dracaena draco*, closely related to the yucca – has barely evolved since the age of the dinosaurs. It has long been an object of fascination, not just among modern botanists and naturalists, but among all who are sensitive to magic and mystery. That's partly because of its curious form, growing like a bundle of separate trunks clinging together before bursting asunder to create the *drago*'s distinctive mushroom shape. Weirdest of all is the *drago*'s strange resin, which turns as red as blood on contact with the air. Though nothing is known of Guanche beliefs, many people insist that the *drago* was worshipped by these first inhabitants of the island, who did use its resin for embalming.

Standing 16m high and with a diameter of 6m, the Drago Milenario is the main attraction at Icod de los Vinos, an attractive little wine town on the west coast. One of Tenerife's largest Guanche settlements stood here when the Europeans arrived, and the Drago Milenario was already mature when the Spanish took control. Alongside an immense palm, the gigantic tree dominates Plaza de la Iglesia, where bars and souvenir shops cash in on the tree's mystique. Different from the rest, and an attraction in itself, is the traditional and pretty shop, Casa del Drago.

 28B4

Plaza de la Iglesia, Icod de los Vinos

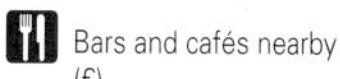

Bars and cafés nearby (£)

Nos 354 and 363 (Puerto de la Cruz–Icod) every 30 mins

Icod de los Vinos (➤ 64), Garachico (➤ 20)

Icod holds a Dragon Tree Festival in September

3
El Teide

28C3

Heart of the Parque Nacional del Teide, access from southeast

Nearest eating places are the *parador* and the Restaurante Boca del Tauce, at the Boca del Tauce junction 10km south

Route 348 runs from Puerto de la Cruz to the Teide *teleférico* once daily, leaving Puerto at 9:15 and reaching the cable car at 11:15. The return trip is at 4:15. Route 342 runs from Playa de las Américas to Teide cable car once daily, leaving Playa at 9:15 and arriving at the cable car at 11:15. The return trip is at 3:40

None

By cable car: expensive. On foot: free

Parque Nacional del Teide (► 66)

The highest mountain in all Spain is an active – but sleeping – volcano, soaring majestically above the Atlantic island it helped to create.

Mount Teide was aflame as Christopher Columbus passed this way. The sailors took it for an ill omen, Columbus for a good one. It could erupt again at any time, though for a century or so at a stretch the volcano remains dormant, its occasional murmurings no more threatening than the purring of a sleeping lion. The most recent eruption was a small one in 1898, and El Teide has been very quiet since. Before the Spanish conquest, the Guanche people of the Canaries – not just on Tenerife but the other islands too – revered and worshipped this conical mountain crested with snow and fire. Even today, El Teide's awesome aloofness gives a sense of the power of the cosmos.

Over the millennia, El Teide's eruptions have added more and more land to the island of Tenerife, though the terrain all around the volcano is a blasted landscape of twisted rock and debris, a devastation that thrills and amazes visitors. This region now has protected status within the Parque Nacional del Teide (► 66). Although not an attraction, not an entertainment, not even particularly accessible, and offering nothing but its dignified presence, El Teide ranks first among the 'must sees' of Tenerife.

Curiously, El Teide is a mere remnant of the original Tenerife volcano, the cone of which at some point blew itself to pieces in a massive eruption. The relics of the cone surround El Teide in a ring of lesser volcanic outlets which are known as the Caldera de las Cañadas.

The 3,718m-high mountain does not always permit people to visit, guarding its privacy in mist, snow or powerful winds – sometimes even when the weather is perfect down on the coast. In the height of summer, heat can be a problem, often reaching 40°C. However, on finer days the summit can be reached either on foot in around three hours or, more usual, by *teleférico* (cable car) in eight minutes. The cable car can, however, involve long waits (over an hour is not unusual), and still leaves a final steep 25-minute scramble on loose scree to reach the very peak,

which rises a tough 170m above the terminal. To do this last bit you will need a permit (see panel, right).

A single well-worn footpath makes its way to the summit from the car park below Montaña Blanca, close to the lower cable car terminal. Only experienced walkers, properly equipped, should attempt any other route. It is easier to walk up than down, so consider taking the cable car one way. The path first climbs Montaña Blanca, which you may consider rewarding enough by itself. Bear in mind that altitude sickness may be a problem, so go slowly to minimise this risk.

On this final climb to the top, there's a whiff of sulphur in the air and a real sense that El Teide means business. You pass impressive smoke holes some 50m across. Take this climb gently, carry some water with you, wear a sunhat and dark glasses, and carry a light sweater to wear at the summit. Whether by foot or by *teleférico*, the view is dramatic and the experience unforgettable.

Above: *a view of El Teide with Los Roques de Garcia in the foreground*
Left: *a cable car approaches the summit of El Teide*

Permits to climb the last 170m to the peak from the cable car station are availble from the Park office in Santa Cruz ✉ 5 Calle Calzadilla, by Plaza España 🕓 Mon–Fri 9–2. Take the passports of everybody who will be going

4

Garachico

28B4

Isla Baja (££) for fish, Bodegón Plaza (£) and Casa Ramón (£) serve Canarian dishes

No 363 (Puerto de la Cruz–Buenavista) hourly stops here

None

Icod de los Vinos (▶ 64), Drago Milenario (▶ 17)

Romería de San Roque (▶ 116), Feria Artesanía (craft fair) first Sun, monthly

For the very best view of the lava flow that engulfed Garachico, take the mountain road (TF1421) up to **Mirador de Garachico**

Above: *the fortress of San Miguel stands guard above the sea*

Convento de San Francisco

Plaza Glorieta de San Francisco

Mon–Fri 9–7, Sat 9–6, Sun 9–1

None

Moderate

Castillo de San Miguel

922 83 00 00

Daily 9–6

None

Cheap

For 200 years, vessels set sail laden with wine and sugar from Garachico, Tenerife's busiest port. Then in one night – Garachico was destroyed.

Created as a port by Genoese entrepreneur Cristobal de Ponte in 1496, the original Garachico became a prosperous colonial town and so it remained for two centuries. Today it lies partly buried beneath today's town – on 5 May 1706 the Volcan Negra (just south of the town) roared into life, pouring lava through Garachico and into its harbour.

The islanders laid out new streets on the land formed by the lava. But the harbour – originally much larger – was never to recover, and Garachico, with its fine mansions and cobbled streets, became a handsome relic.

Around main square Plaza Glorieta de San Francisco, the old Franciscan monastery, **Convento de San Francisco**, pre-dates the eruption. It now houses the Casa de Cultura, which hosts events and exhibitions (go inside just to see the pretty interiors and two courtyards), and the Museo de las Ciencias Naturales, a modest mix of local flora, fauna and history. Don't miss the pictures showing the route of the lava flow.

Parque Puerto de Tierra, a lush sunken gardens alongside Plaza de Juan González de la Torre, was part of Garachico's harbour. A huge arch which marked the port entrance has been dug out of the lava and re-erected in the square, while close by an enormous wine press also pre-dates the eruption.

For a tremendous view, go up to the roof of **Castillo de San Miguel**. This dark 16th-century fortress of the Counts of Gomera, emblazoned with their crests, stood firm as the lava flowed past. Today it contains a little museum and craft stall. Steps lead down to the sea, where the lava has made pleasing rocky pools.

5
Loro Parque, Puerto de la Cruz

The number one family attraction on Tenerife is a tropical wildlife park that mixes conservation, education, entertainment and fun.

This is one of the original tourist attractions on Tenerife, located in the island's first holiday resort. From simple beginnings in 1972 as a Parrot Park (which is what Loro Parque means), today it's an internationally acclaimed award-winning wildlife theme park, an extravaganza of tropical gardens, a dolphinarium and sea life centre with many related attractions and rides. Covering 12.5ha, with over 2,000 palm trees, it's home to a colony of gorillas, and has a water zone where the ever-popular sea lions and dolphins seem to relish their role as a holiday entertainment. The Park's aquarium tunnel, believed to be the longest in the world, is a transparent underwater walkway 18.5m long. As you walk along, sharks slip through the water, just a few centimetres away. There are flamingos, crocodiles, cranes, giant turtles, jaguars, monkeys and a Nocturnal Bat Cave. The latest addition is Planet Penguin. A special effects cinema, Natura Vision, takes you on a trip through other wildlife centres around the world.

Parrots, however, remain an important element of the Park. There are over 300 species living here – the world's largest collection. The birds are being studied, and the Park is engaged in important breeding and conservation work. While endangered parrot species may be confined, the more common varieties are used in parrot shows several times each day. These feature clever tricks and elaborate entertainments which the parrots have learned to perform.

 28C4

  3km west of town near Punta Brava

 922 37 38 41

Daily 8:30–5

Choice of places within the Park, including a pizzeria (££) and a self-service buffet (£)

Free shuttle bus from Avenida de Venezuela (near Lido) and Plaza del Charco, Puerto de la Cruz

Plaza de la Iglesia
922 38 60 00

Few

Very expensive

Puerto de la Cruz (► 54)

The attractions of Loro Parque extend to many more species in addition to the parrots

6
Los Gigantes

28A3

43km from Playa de las Américas; take the coast road to Puerto de Santiago, and continue 2km beyond it

Several tourist bars and restaurants in the resort of Los Gigantes (£–££)

No 473 runs to the other south coast resorts

Excursions from Puerto de Santiago, Playa de las Américas and Los Cristianos

None

Garachico (► 20), El Teide (► 18)

The black sand beach at Puerto de Santiago

These stupendous sheer cliffs are called The Giants, an apt description of the rockface, which soars to a dramatic 600m from blue sea to the blue sky.

One of Tenerife's most breathtaking sights is best seen from a boat: properly known as Acantilado de los Gigantes, the soaring dark rock-face rising 500m from the Atlantic waves marks the abrupt edge of northwestern Tenerife's Teno Massif. There's nothing more to the site but its sheer grandeur, but that's enough to attract almost all visitors to Tenerife. Come by car or coach and join a sightseeing boat when you arrive, or, perhaps better, many excursions come by boat all the way from the resorts. Either way, it's not until you see another boat cruising gently at the foot of these cliffs that their true majesty becomes clear.

The cliffs rise from one end of a pleasant bay called La Canalita. At the other end of the curve of sandy bay, there's a small resort area with a quiet, civilised feel and a black sand beach to call its own. Being slightly remote, it manages to preserve a calm holiday atmosphere now rare on the island. The cliffs and the sea guarantee that this little resort cannot expand much.

Just 1km away (as the crow flies), Puerto de Santiago is a larger purpose-built resort which has sprung up beside a small fishing harbour village and a good black sand beach. The village adds a measure of charm to an otherwise rather bland resort, popular with the British.

7

Mercado Nuestra Señora de África, Santa Cruz

Tenerife's main produce market, the market of Our Lady of Africa, is a dazzle of colour and energy, a picture of the island's abundance.

35C2

Calle de San Sebastián, Santa Cruz

Mon–Sat 8–1 (Sun *rastro* market 10–2)

The generosity of the Canaries and their surrounding ocean, and their ready access to all the abundance of the rest of Spain, are daily apparent in the wonderful displays in this lively and atmospheric enclosed marketplace. Flowers fill the eye, alongside the colours of myriad fruits and vegetables. Other stalls are laden with fish and meat. You'll find small live animals, a multitude of curious peasant cheeses made of cows', sheep's or goats' milk (or sometimes all three) and home-made honey. Here too are the traders selling cheap cassettes and CDs – often of foot-stamping Spanish and Latin American music. Interestingly, all is neat and orderly, with a surprising tidiness and efficiency.

The market is located near the heart of the oldest quarter of Tenerife's capital town, not far from the lanes of a red-light district, and usually spills out into these surrounding streets, where stalls sell 'dry goods' – kitchenware, fabrics and household items. The market entrance itself is a circular arch, leading straight into the flower-stall area. Beyond lies a veritable bazaar of stalls within the central courtyard.

There's officially no market here on Sunday, but that's when the big weekly *rastro* sets up outside the market hall. A *rastro* is a mixed flea market and craft market, where an array of stallholders from home and abroad sell a hotch-potch of cheap souvenirs, second-rate factory-made 'craft' items, leather goods, assorted cast-offs and secondhand items, as well as plenty of genuine high-quality arts and crafts. Philatelists will love it: stamps are a particular speciality of several stallholders.

Plaza de España, Santa Cruz 922 60 58 00 Mon–Sat 8–3 (in summer, Mon–Fri 8–2, Sat 9–1)

Few

Santa Cruz (► 32)

Watch out for pickpockets! Tourists at the market are seen as easy prey

Above: *visitors to the market are greeted by a glorious array of flowers*

8

Museo Etnográfico de Tenerife, Casa de Carta

The graceful white-painted exterior of the Casa de Carta

A fascinating collection of Canary Islands folk culture, housed in a fine restored country mansion, one of the most beautiful buildings on the island.

29D5

44 Carretera Tacoronte–Valle de Guerra, 25km from Puerto de la Cruz. Take North freeway, then Guamasa exit to Valle Guerra intersection and to Boqueron via Valle Guerra

922 54 30 53

Tue–Sat 10–8, Sun 10–2

In and around nearby Tacoronte (££)

Call Tacoronte Bus Information on 922 56 18 07 for bus times

None

Moderate

El Sauzal (► 44)

This beautiful, low, white-painted Canarian farmhouse and country mansion dates back to the end of the 17th century, and is one of Tenerife's prettiest architectural gems. Faultlessly restored, the building is an exquisite arrangement of carved wooden doors, balconies, porticos and patios. It stands among tropical gardens in the countryside overlooking the village of Valle de Guerra.

For centuries the home of the Carta family of regional administrators, the casa now houses the important Tenerife Ethnographic Museum. Reconstructed rooms reveal much about life in rural Tenerife, and there are examples of all the island's ancestral crafts and folk arts and crafts. Inside, 14 exhibition rooms with their galleries are used to re-create appealing little glimpses of ordinary life in the rural Tenerife of past times. The principal displays are of weaving, needlework and pottery, as well as farm tools, fabrics, clothing, ceramics and furniture.

The most interesting exhibits are of Canary Islands traditional dress from the 18th century onwards, highlighting the small but important differences of style and colour between one island and the next. Embroidered and patterned festival clothes, wedding clothes and everyday workwear are on show. The weaving and sewing rooms show how these clothes would have been made in those earlier days.

9

Nuestra Señora de la Concepción, La Laguna

When Guanche leaders were 'persuaded' to become Christian and submit to Spanish rule, they were brought to this grandiose church to be baptised.

The oldest church on the island, with much outstanding craftsmanship, Our Lady of the Immaculate Conception represents a landmark in Canarian history and has the status of a Spanish national shrine. Its greatest claim to fame is that the big glazed 16th-century baptismal font, brought here from Seville in southern Spain, was used to 'convert' defeated Guanche warriors to Christianity. You'll find it in the *baptisterie* (baptistery) set to one side of the main entrance, with family trees displayed above.

Though much changed since, even in those days the church was extraordinarily grand for a far-flung new colony, with elaborately carved gilded wooden ceiling panels in Moorish design. Over the centuries, the church benefited from the finest workmanship on the island, its Gothic origins becoming overlaid with Renaissance style and then gaudy baroque decoration.

First built in 1502, the triple-naved church has probably the grandest and richest interior on Tenerife, and rivals any other building in the Canaries. The gold and silver paintwork and metalwork are breathtaking, together with rich retables from the 17th century and later. Immediately obvious on entering the building, the extravagant woodcarving of the 18th-century pulpit is considered one of Spain's best examples of this type of work. The choir stalls, too, are beautifully carved.

The eye-catching seven-storey tower, dating from the 17th century, has a distinctive Moorish look and is the principal landmark of this historic town.

The side altar leads the eye upwards with its ascending gilded tiers

29E5

Calle Obispo Rey Redondo

Usually Mon–Fri 10–12, Sat–Sun services only

Nearby tapas bars and restaurants, eg Tasca La Carpentaría (££)

No 102 (Puerto de la Cruz or Santa Cruz–La Laguna) every 30 mins

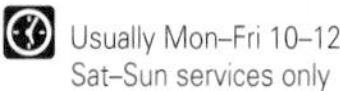

Few

Cheap

La Laguna (➤ 45)

➤ 116 for dates of festivals in La Laguna

10

Parque Nacional de Garajonay, La Gomera

82B2

Enter the Park via the Visitor Centre at Juego de Bolas, see below, or on rough minor roads and tracks from other villages

Restaurant at La Laguna Grande (££)

Nearest: La Gomera Island Tourist Board, 4 Calle Real, San Sebastián de la Gomera
922 14 01 47

None

Free

Agulo (► 84), Chipude (► 84), Hermingua (► 85)

The tiny woodland chapel of the Ermitage de Nuestra Señora de Lourdes, near the village of El Cedro on the east side of the Park, is the destination for an annual forest pilgrimage on the last Sun in Aug

Visitor Centre

Juego de Bolas, near Las Rosas (35km from San Sebastián)

922 80 09 93

Tue–Sun 9:30–4:30. The craft workshops are open Tue–Fri only

Few

Free

A vast area of protected Canarian forest covers the central upland of La Gomera: a strange, dark wilderness of lichens, ravines and laurel canyons.

While sun beats down on the southern shore, a cooler, damper climate prevails around Mount Garajonay. Heather, ferns and lichens flourish, creating a thick carpet across the boulders and rocky slopes where the last of the original Canarian laurel woodland survives. Waterfalls and streams splash through the greenery. Walking in this wet, magical terrain among the slender, sinuous limbs of the Canary laurel (*Larus canariensis*), it is certainly hard to believe that you are in the Canary Islands. Not just laurel but also the luxuriant Canary date palm (*Phoenix canariensis*) grows here in great numbers, and there are around 400 species of native flowers, some found only at this place. There are, too, many rare insects and birds.

First stop before exploring should be the **Centro de Visitantes (Visitor Centre)** at Juego de Bolas, on the north side of the forest. This gives an overview of the Park and its flora and fauna, and details all the marked forest walks. The Centre has much else of interest about La Gomera, including gardens, a small museum, and displays about island life over the centuries. Craftspeople demonstrate traditional skills such as weaving, pottery, basketmaking and carpentry.

Easy, popular walks start at La Laguna Grande centre, in the middle of the forest, where there's a woodland play area, a board showing marked trails, and a track up to a lofty *mirador* (viewpoint) from which you can see Tenerife.

Sunlight reaches between the trees to the flowers covering the forest floor

What to See

Above: *palms form a striking pattern on the beach at Playa de las Teresitas*
Right: *a bronze statue near the Palacio Insular in Plaza de España*

TENERIFE

5

4

Ja Bot
Pue la
Loro Parque
Bananera el G
La O
San Juan de la Ramba
Punta del Casado
Roque de Garachico
San Marcos
Mirador de Don Pompeyo
Buenavista del Norte
Castillo de San Miguel
Garachico
Icod de los Vinos
La Guancha
Icod El Alto
Los Realejo
Los Silos
El Tanque
Drago Milenario
Macizo de Teno
Punta de Teno
Teno
La Portela
Val
1626m
Volcán Negro
El Portillo
Masca
Santiago del Teide
Cueva del Hielo
Centro de Visitantes

3

3718m
El Teide
Altavista
2750m
Montaña Blanca
Tamaimo
Arguayo
Las Narices del Teide
Las Lavas Negras
Parque Nacional del Teide
Las Cañadas
Los Gigantes
Puerto de Santiago
Chio
Los Roques de García
Parador Nacional de las Cañadas
Llano de Ucanca
Boca del Tauce
Alcalá
Guía de Isora
Paisaje Lunar
San Juan
Tejina
Campame del Mad

2

Taucho
Marazul
Barranco del Infierno
Vilaflor
Callao Salvaje
Armeñime
Playa Paraiso
Casa Fuerte
Adeje
Valle de San Lorenzo
Grana de Ab
La Caleta
Parque Exóticos
Arona
San Miguel
Aguapark Octopus
Valle de San Lorenzo
Costa Adeje
Mirador de la Centinela
Playa de las Américas
Tenerife Zoo & Monkey Park
Parque Ecológico las Aguilas del Teide
Jardines del Atlántico Bananera
Aer Rei
Los Cristianos
Playa de los Cristianos
Guaza
Karting Club Tenerife
Golf del Sur
El

1

Palm-Mar
Los Abrigos
Ten-Bel
Punta de la Rasca
Las Galletas
Costa del Silencio

A B C

Punta del Hidalgo
Punta del Hidalgo
Chinamada
Taganana
Punta de Anaga
Bajamar
Las Carboneras
Mirador El Bailadero
Mirador Cruz del Carmen
Parque Rural de Anaga
Tejina
Valle Guerra
Tegueste
Mirador Pico del Inglés
Las Montañas de Anaga
Igueste
Museo Etnográfico de Tenerife
Bosque de las Mercedes
Mirador de Jardina
San Andrés
Playa de las Teresitas
Mesa del Mar
Guamasa
Las Canteras
Nuestra Señora de la Concepción
El Sauzal
Tacoronte
La Laguna
Club Nautico
Aeropuerto de Los Rodeos
La Cuesta
SANTA CRUZ DE TENERIFE
La Matanza de Acentejo
La Esperanza
Taco
Mirador Pico de las Flores
Bosque de la Esperanza
Santa Úrsula
Montaña Grande
Las Raíces
Mirador de los Cumbres
Radazul
Tabaiba
Mirador Ortuño
Las Caletillas
Candelaria
Basilica de Nuestra Señora de Candelaria
Arafo
Güimar
Mirador de Don Martín
Puerto de Güimar
Fasnia
Fondeadero de Fasnia
Arico
Poris de Abona
Punta de Abona
Playa del Medio

0 5 10 15 20 km

D E F

The North

The real life of the island is all in the north. Here the whole history of Tenerife can be told, for the Guanches mainly occupied the northern half, and the Spanish too settled and cultivated this area. Until the package holiday boom took off in the 1960s, even holiday-makers rarely ventured south of Puerto de la Cruz, except for the essential excursion to El Teide. As a result, almost all of the island's art, culture, its Spanish colonial legacy, and its best sightseeing, are here.

It was the climate that caused this; the north and northwest, facing the trade winds, catch all of Tenerife's gentle rain. Parts of this fertile half of the island are exotically verdant, with tropical flowers and greenery. That's what attracted the first aristocratic tourists, who adored the permanent springtime, rich crops and garden landscape of northern Tenerife.

'They make wine better than any in Spaine, they have grapes of such bignesse that they may bee compared to damsons; for sugar, suckets, raisins of the Sunne, and many other fruits, abundance.'

RICHARD HAKLUYT,
Principal Navigations (1598–1600)

The glowing altarpiece in the Iglesia de Nuestra Señora de la Concepción, Santa Cruz

Santa Cruz de Tenerife

Santa Cruz, the island's capital, still has the authentic feel and look of colonial Spain. It's not a holiday resort, but a vibrant Latin city where most *Tinerfeños* live and work. The name means Holy Cross of Tenerife, and comes from the crucifix planted boldly at this spot by the ruthless Spanish conqueror Alonso Fernández de Lugo, when he strode ashore in 1494 with 1,000 men to take possession of the Guanches' island home.

Above: *crowds throng one of the principal shopping streets in the centre of Santa Cruz*

Right: *the whitewashed façade of the Iglesia de San Francisco*

During the five centuries since the conquest, Santa Cru has remained the focal point of Tenerife's religion, cultur and history. While the gaudy, multicultural Tenerife o modern tourism stays way down south, the resolutel Spanish capital has remained almost unaffected by th millions of package holiday visitors. That's partly due t climate: most of the island's scant rain falls on this stretc of coast, so only tourists determined to know and under stand the island, and looking for something more than suntan, would choose to stay here. It's also due to th diverse economy of the capital, with its oil processing waterfront industry and deep-water harbour. Not only di this make the town uninterested in tourism, but to som extent it made tourists uninterested in the town. No though, Santa Cruz has polished up some of its treasure and even provides a jaunty little 'train' to take people on tour of the sights. At the same time, holidaymakers hav realised there's more to Tenerife than suntan lotion bierkellers and crowded black beaches, and that much c the best sightseeing is in and around Santa Cruz.

What to see in Santa Cruz

IGLESIA DE NUESTRA SEÑORA DE LA CONCEPCIÓN (CHURCH OF OUR LADY OF THE CONCEPTION)

One of the city's most important landmarks, this church is also one of its most significant historical monuments. Its attractive square tower rises from an open plaza enclosed by whitewashed 19th-century buildings (including the handsome exterior of the tobacco works, Tinerfeña Fabrica de Tabacos). Built in 1502, much changed in the 17th and 18th centuries, the church was reopened in 1999 after many years of being closed for restoration. The cross which de Lugo first placed on Tenerife soil has been kept here for centuries, as has the British flag captured from one of Nelson's ships during the 1797 raid. An additional feature of this fine church is the tomb of Nelson's opponent, General Gutierrez, defender of Santa Cruz.

35D2
Plaza de la Iglesia
Daily
Nearby in Plaza de la Candelaria (££)
None
Free

IGLESIA DE SAN FRANCISCO (CHURCH OF ST FRANCIS)

This delightful church combines simplicity with elaborate, abundant decoration. Most striking are the ceiling of wooden beams, the painted arch, a fine organ and two baroque *retablos* (altarpieces) dating from the 17th and 18th centuries. To the right of the high altar is a separate chapel with a Moorish-style ceiling. The church, built in 1680, was originally part of the Franciscan monastery of San Pedro de Alcántara, said to have been founded by Irish refugees fleeing from Elizabeth I's anti-Catholic tyranny. The monastery no longer exists, but the buildings now house the Municipal Fine Arts Museum (➤ 37); the square in which it stands was once the friary garden.

35C3
Plaza del Príncipe
Daily
Café del Príncipe (£–££) in Plaza del Príncipe
None
Free
Museo Municipal de Bellas Artes (➤ 37)

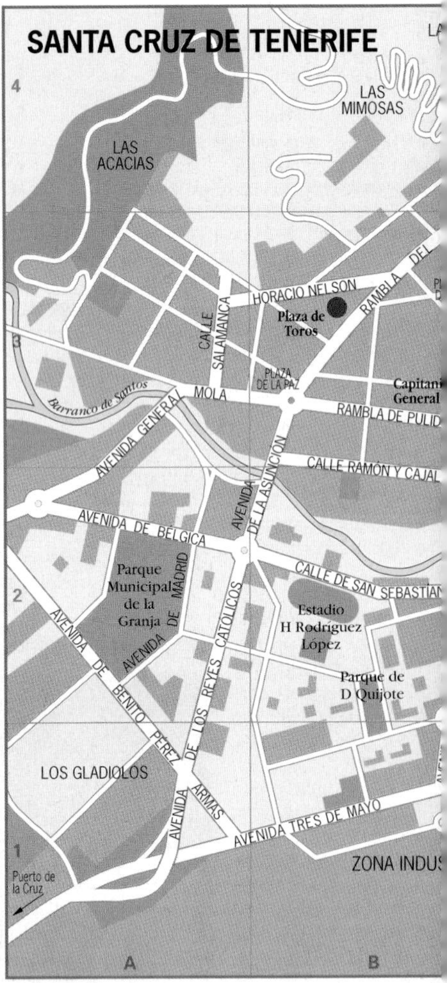

SANTA CRUZ DE TENERIFE

LAS MIMOSAS
LAS ACACIAS
HORACIO NELSON
RAMBLA DEL
Plaza de Toros
CALLE SALAMANCA
PLAZA DE LA PAZ
Capitanía General
MOLA
Barranco de Santos
RAMBLA DE PULIDO
AVENIDA GENERAL
CALLE RAMÓN Y CAJAL
AVENIDA DE LA ASUNCIÓN
AVENIDA DE BÉLGICA
CALLE DE SAN SEBASTIÁN
Parque Municipal de la Granja
AVENIDA DE MADRID
Estadio H Rodríguez López
AVENIDA DE BENITO PÉREZ
AVENIDA DE LOS REYES CATÓLICOS
Parque de D Quijote
LOS GLADIOLOS
ARMAS
AVENIDA TRES DE MAYO
ZONA INDUS
Puerto de la Cruz
A
B
1
2
3
4

Above: *the massive Monumento de los Caidos in Plaza de España, set against the Palacio Insular*

Right: *the Plaza de la Candelaria, a popular pedestrianised shopping area in Santa Cruz*

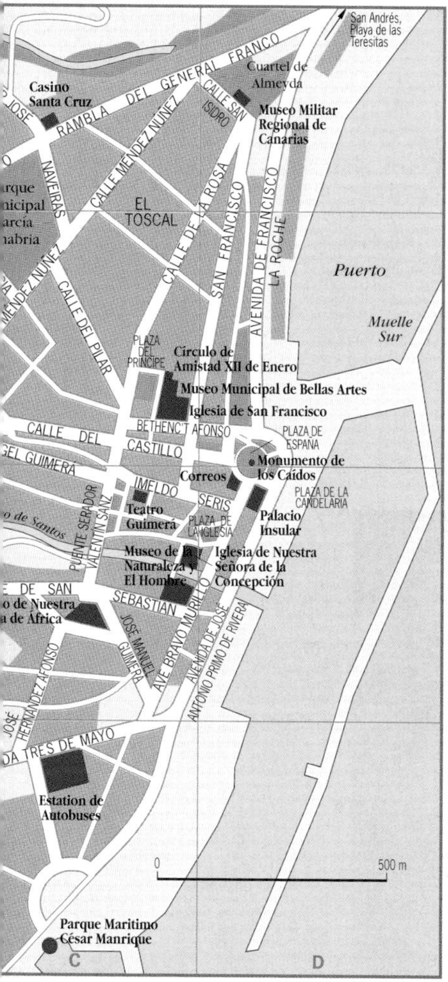

San Andrés, Playa de las Teresitas
RAMBLA DEL GENERAL FRANCO
Cuartel de Almeyda
Casino Santa Cruz
CALLE SAN ISIDRO
Museo Militar Regional de Canarias
CALLE MENDEZ NUÑEZ
NAVEIRAS
EL TOSCAL
CALLE DE LA ROSA
SAN FRANCISCO
AVENIDA DE FRANCISCO LA ROCHE
Puerto
Muelle Sur
CALLE DEL PILAR
PLAZA DEL PRINCIPE
Circulo de Amistad XII de Enero
Museo Municipal de Bellas Artes
Iglesia de San Francisco
BETHENC'T AFONSO
PLAZA DE ESPAÑA
CALLE DEL CASTILLO
Monumento de los Caídos
Correos
IMELDO SERIS
PLAZA DE LA CANDELARIA
Teatro Guimerá
PLAZA DE LA IGLESIA
Palacio Insular
PUENTE SERADOR
VALENTIN SANZ
Museo de la Naturaleza y El Hombre
Iglesia de Nuestra Señora de la Concepción
SAN SEBASTIAN
JOSÉ MANUEL GUIMERA
AVE BRAVO MURILLO
AVENIDA DE JOSÉ ANTONIO PRIMO DE RIVERA
JOSÉ HERNANDEZ AFONSO
TRES DE MAYO
Estation de Autobuses
0
500 m
Parque Maritimo César Manrique
C
D

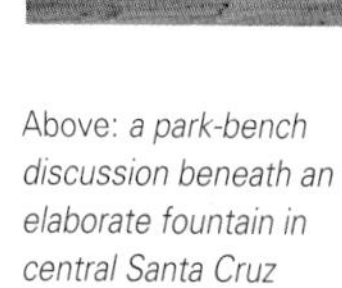

Above: *a park-bench discussion beneath an elaborate fountain in central Santa Cruz*

Left: *busts adorn the exterior of the Museo Municipal de Bellas Artes, in Plaza del Príncipe*

Around Santa Cruz

Distance
3km

Time
1 hour walking, plus 2 hours sightseeing

Start/end point
Plaza de España
35D3

Lunch
Café del Príncipe (££)
Plaza del Príncipe
922 27 88 10

Start at the tourist office, in the waterfront Plaza de España, dominated by its Civil War memorial and its Palacio Insular (► 40).

Walk into the adjoining square, Plaza de la Candelaria.

This agreeable pedestrianised square (► 40) has good bars, craft shops and sights, including the Banco Español de Credito in the charming 18th-century Palacio de Carta.

At the end of the square, continue on Calle del Castillo.

This is the main shopping street of Santa Cruz, a lively, colourful avenue of little shops with gaudy signs, 'bazaars' and mingled crowds of tourists and locals.

Continue to Plaza de Weyler.

There's an Italian white marble fountain at the centre of this popular square. To one side stands the Capitania General, where Franco lived while he was based here.

At the northern tip of the square, turn along Calle Méndez Núñez.

This less interesting street soon leads to the Parque Municipal García Sanabria (► 39), an enjoyable place to get away from street noise and relax on the tiled public benches among greenery.

Take Calle del Pilar, opposite the park's south side. Follow this street to Plaza del Príncipe.

In the slightly raised square, once the friary garden of a Franciscan monastery, luxuriant laurel trees shade a bandstand. To one side the Municipal Fine Arts Museum (► 37) occupies the former monastery, alongside its church, the Iglesia de San Francisco (► 33).

Calle de Béthencourt leads the short distance back to Plaza de España.

An opportunity to rest in the shade at Parque Municipal García Sanabria

MERCADO DE NUESTRA SEÑORA DE ÁFRICA (➤ 23, TOP TEN)

MUSEO MILITAR REGIONAL DE CANARIAS (CANARIES REGIONAL MILITARY MUSEUM)

Todo por la Patria – All for the Fatherland – is the inscription above the gateway into this collection of important relics from the military past of the Canary Islands. Housed in part of the semicircular 19th-century barracks, Cuartel del Almeida, the museum is proud and patriotic in tone. The oldest exhibits are the simple weapons used by the Guanches against the Spanish. Among various later insignia and memorabilia, a highlight of the collection is the cannon called El Tigre, used to defend Santa Cruz against Nelson's 1797 attack and believed to be responsible for the loss of his right arm. Flags taken from Nelson's defeated ship, HMS *Emerald*, are also displayed. Even more compelling is the small section devoted to General Francisco Franco, dictator of Spain from 1936 to 1975. Here visitors can see his desk, plans and a photograph of Franco with supporters pledging allegiance at *Las Raíces* (The Roots), near La Esperanza. A map shows the route of the plane *Dragon Rapide*, which flew from Croydon in southern England to Tenerife, picked up the future dictator and took him to Morocco, from where he launched his coup.

35D4
Calle San Isidro 2
922 27 16 62
Tue–Sun 10–1:30
None
Cheap
Parque Municipal García Sanabria (➤ 39)
Remember to take your passport to the Muséo Militar – you probably won't be admitted without it!

El Tigre is famed as the cannon that was fired on the occasion when Nelson lost his arm

MUSEO MUNICIPAL DE BELLAS ARTES (MUNICIPAL FINE ARTS MUSEUM)

It comes as a surprise, perhaps, that Tenerife's excellent Municipal Fine Arts Museum was opened in 1900, long before the tourism boom. Together with the city library, it is housed in the pleasant setting of a former Franciscan monastery. The 10 busts lined up outside are of Tenerife artists, musicians, writers and thinkers. Inside, an eclectic collection on two storeys includes the work of Canarian artists, several of historical interest, and more distinguished European works mainly covering the 17th–19th centuries. Most interesting are the successive temporary exhibitions of art works loaned by Spain's leading museums of art.

35C3
Calle José Murphy 4, Plaza del Príncipe
922 24 43 58
Mon–Fri 10–8
Café del Príncipe (££)
Few
Free
Iglesia de San Francisco (➤ 33)

- 35C2
- Calle Fuentes Morales (the main entrance is on the Iglesia de NS de la Concepción side)
- General information: 922 20 93 20, Archaeology: 922 20 93 17, Natural Sciences: 922 20 93 14
- Tue–Sun 10–8 (last tickets are sold at 7PM)
- Nearby in Plaza de la Candelaria
- 10 minutes' walk from Central Bus Station
- Very good
- Cheap
- Iglesia de Nuestra Señora de la Concepción (► 33)

Above: *the attractive verandas of the Museo de la Naturaleza y el Hombre*

MUSEO DE LA NATURALEZA Y EL HOMBRE (MUSEUM OF NATURE AND MAN) ✪✪✪

This extraordinary museum, situated in a most attractive former hospital with an inner galleried courtyard, deals seriously but accessibly with the archaeology, anthropology and ethnography of the Canaries, as well as the islands' natural history. The museum is essentially two museums in one – Nature and Man being dealt with separately – and is split in half, naturally following the shape of the building. Archaeology and the human life of the Canaries lie on the left of the entrance and the fauna and flora of the islands on the right. Ten distinct sections tackle these different aspects of the Canary Islands with displays as varied as African and pre-Columbian art, aboriginal therapy, the Canaries during the Spanish Conquest and the Canary Islands today.

The main emphasis is placed on the islands' pre-Hispanic history and culture. Much of the evidence of Guanche culture relates to burial, and the museum displays fascinating material on Guanche tombs and burial sites. Some dramatic exhibits include Guanche preserved bodies in a display on mummification, as well as skeletons and hundreds of skulls, some of them trepanned (with drilled holes). Interesting too, though less dramatic, are the displays of Guanche household items, pottery, tools and body decorations, as well as indigenous Canarian plant and animal life.

- 35C1
- Castillo de San Juan (off Avenida de José Antonio Primo de Rivera, 1km south of Plaza de España)
- 922 20 32 44
- Daily 10–5
- Choice on site (£–£££)
- Frequent town buses along Avenida de José Antonio Primo de Rivera
- Few
- Cheap
- Mercado de Nuestra Señora de África (► 23)

PARQUE MARÍTIMO CÉSAR MANRIQUE (CÉSAR MANRIQUE MARINE PARK) ✪✪✪

When the Cabildo (Island Council) of Tenerife wanted to do something with the unsightly disused industrial dockyards near the old Castillo de San Juan, they commissioned the brilliant Canarian artist and designer César Manrique to create something for them. Believing passionately that tourism would be the salvation of the Canaries if carefully controlled, but would destroy the islands if given free rein, Manrique had already created several exceptionally imaginative tourist sites on his native Lanzarote. Most of Lanzarote's success and style (and its strict planning laws) were due entirely to this one man. At Santa Cruz his brief was limited, but even so Manrique managed to redesign the docklands site into an attractive leisure complex linking

the sea with the Castillo. The Castillo dates back to 1641, and was one of two main defences for the town (the other was Castillo San Cristóbal, located where Plaza de España lies now).

Much of the design has not yet been enacted, but today the Parque Marítimo is a delightful lido, with palms and sunbathing terraces around a beautiful seawater pool (similar to the lido César Manrique created for Puerto de la Cruz, ► 60). Eventually it should include a cultural centre, a folk museum, a maritime museum, exhibition halls and other leisure facilities, all within the aesthetic and constrained style of Manrique's original plan.

Below: *Park Marítimo César Manrique features a large and imaginatively designed swimming pool*

PARQUE MUNICIPAL GARCÍA SANABRIA ✪✪

This delightful 6-hectare park full of shrubs, trees, exotic flowers, fountains and tranquil corners is the largest – and probably the most beautiful – urban park in the Canaries. Popular with locals, it was laid out in the 1920s, and is named after the mayor of that time. He is honoured by a large monument in the centre of the park. Odd, slightly incongruous pieces of modern sculpture dotted about are the product of an international street sculpture competition held in 1973, and there's a zoo, a play area and an intriguing floral clock. Take a break on the tiled public benches, stroll the gravel pathways or get a snack at one of the little kiosks.

- 35C3
- Entered from Calle Méndez Núñez
- Snacks available at park kiosks (£)
- Town buses along Rambla del General Franco
- Few
- Free
- Museo Municipal de Bellas Artes (► 37), Iglesia de San Francisco (► 33)

35D2
Adjacent to Plaza de España
Several bars and cafés in the square (£–££)

PLAZA DE LA CANDELARIA 

This pleasant traffic-free square has good bars and shops, including an *artesanía* (craft shop). Centuries ago, it was the entrance to the vanished Castillo San Cristóbal, once one of the two main defences of the town (the other was Castillo San Juan), and here the island's troops would parade and be inspected. The centrepiece of the plaza is the appealing baroque statue of Our Lady of Candelaria, holding the infant Jesus and a tall candle. Formerly known as Plaza del Castillo, the square acquired its new name along with the statue.

At No 9, the Banco Español de Credito occupies the old Palacio de Carta: behind a rather dull façade this is a fine 18th-century mansion with carved wooden balconies and an elegant patio, immaculately restored by the bank. Originally built as the family home of Captain Matías Carta, it is now one of the best examples of traditional Canarian domestic architecture. Open during bank hours, it deserves a look inside – perhaps when you need to change money.

35D3
Off Avenida de José Antonio Primo de Rivera
Bars and cafés nearby (£–££)

PLAZA DE ESPAÑA 

A large square near the waterfront, this spacious plaza is the heart of the city. The whole square was formerly the site of the principal Santa Cruz fortification, Castillo San Cristóbal, demolished in 1929. Here today stands the grimly imposing Franco-era Palacio Insular, seat of the Island Council, built in what was known as Rationalist style. The huge central Monumento de los Caidos, Monument to the Fallen, honours local people who fell in war, including the Spanish Civil War – Franco's manifesto was broadcast from here. The Monument is flanked by statues of two *menceys* (chieftains).

A somewhat forbidding statue on Monumento de los Caidos

What to See in the North

BAJAMAR ✪

One of the oldest resorts on Tenerife, Bajamar makes a sharp contrast with the glitzier newcomers on the sunny south coast and has a loyal following. Here on the extreme northern shores of the island, constant breezes and turbulent underwater currents stir up the waves onto the black beach. For that reason, bathers rarely venture into the sea. Instead, visitors do most of their swimming and sunbathing at the seashore lido and hotel pools. It's also a quieter, less crowded, less developed holiday environment – precisely what attracts its devotees. Once a fishing village, Bajamar has few signs of its past, and now seems unfocused, with a long promenade and side turns, with many bars, restaurants and shops.

- 29E5
- 15km north of La Laguna
- A wide variety of bars and restaurants (£–££)
- Bus 105 (Santa Cruz–Bajamar) every 30 mins
- Few
- Punta del Hidalgo (➤ 50), La Laguna (➤ 45)

Above: *safe inside the natural swimming pool at Bajamar, swimmers watch the spray outside*

CASA DE CARTA (➤ 24, TOP TEN)

CASA DEL VINO LA BARANDA 

Usually known simply as the Casa del Vino, this superb *bodega* (wine cellar) situated in a converted 17th-century farmhouse makes an enjoyable and educational outing – and a great excuse to stock up on a few bottles of local wine. Payment of a small charge enables visitors to taste any 10 of the 150 wines stocked here. Not simply a shop, it sets out to inform tourists about the range and qualities of Tenerife wines.

For those who want to go deeper into the subject, the Casa houses a small wine museum. It also shows a 10-minute film on the history of wine-making on the island, and explains why here, as in many other wine regions, quality has much improved in recent years. The restaurant (open to all) has panoramic views as well as good food.

- 29D4
- On coast road just south of El Sauzal, 18km east of Puerto de la Cruz
- 922 57 25 35
- Tue–Sat 11–8, Sun and hols 11–6
- Restaurant on site (££) where you can eat without visiting the museum or tasting room
- Buses from Puerto and La Laguna
- Few
- Cheap
- El Sauzal (➤ 44)

In the Know

If you only have a short time to visit Tenerife and would like to get a real flavour of the island, here are some ideas:

10 Ways to Be a Local

Order a *caña* ... not a *cerveza* or *biera* or beer. Best of all, ask for a Dorada, the locally brewed beer.

Ignore the menu In an ordinary restaurant or bar, locals often don't look at the menu – they just ask the waiter what's on offer that day.

Drink espresso If you want coffee have a *solo* (espresso). It's all right to have a little milk in an espresso – ask for a *cortado*. It's OK, though, to have *café con leche* for breakfast.

Take the kids Locals have a simple answer to the babysitter problem – anywhere that a man can take his wife, he can take his kids. Spanish couples take children with them almost everywhere, at almost any time of day or night. There's no bedtime.

Eat *tapas* ... but not before 12 o'clock. *Tapas* are appetisers or between-meals savouries, and should be nibbled with an apéritif during the long, long hours between lunch and dinner.

Eat late Although Canarian mealtimes are not as late as on the mainland, locals often eat lunch at 2PM and dinner at 9PM.

Take a siesta Locals have a long day, with an early start and a late finish. The secret is to slow down after lunch. Draw the curtains, sit quietly and don't leave your room.

Shout Yell every word. In Spanish, of course.

Hold your drink Get tipsy, laugh, talk loudly, be happy after a few glasses of wine – but uncontrolled, rowdy or drunken behaviour is strictly for tourists.

Forget flamenco Big tourist hotels and other venues put on popular Spanish folklore shows for guests, but traditions like flamenco are not part of Canary Islands culture.

5 Top Activities

Dive ➤ 112–113
Whale-watch ➤ 106, 111
Golf ➤ 112
Walk ➤ 113
Go bananas ➤ 55

10 Good Places to Have Lunch

El Patio (£££) Calle Gran Bretaña, Urbanización San Eugenío, Playa de las Américas ☎ 922 79 41 11 The terrace of the hotel-restaurant Jardín Tropical provides among the very best lunchtime experiences on the south coast. Cuisine is high-quality Canarian and mainland Spanish.

El Sol (£££) Calle El Cabezo, Los Cristianos ☎ 922 70 05 69 One of the best places in Los Cristianos for a lunch of Canarian and international cooking, stylishly served.

Jardín Tecina Restaurant (££) Lomada de Tecina, Playa de Santiago, La Gomera ☎ 922 14 58 50

Below: *dedicated golfers increasingly choose Tenerife for holidays*

Enjoy lunch with a superb sea view on this wonderful hotel terrace on the south coast of La Gomera.

La Cava (££) Calle El Cabezo, Los Cristianos
☎ 922 79 04 93
Unusual in this touristy zone, enjoy authentic Spanish cooking in a pleasant outdoor setting.

La Lagostera (£–££) Paseo Maritimo, Los Abrigos
☎ 922 17 03 02
A tempting little fish restaurant where you can enjoy the freshest of simple Canarian cooking.

Los Troncos (££) 17 Calle General Goded, Santa Cruz
☎ 922 28 41 52
One of the very best restaurants in the Tenerife capital, noted for its high standard of Canarian cooking and also for its Basque specialities.

Parador de San Sebastián de la Gomera (££–£££) Balcon de la Villa y Puerto, Lomo de la Horca, San Sebastián, La Gomera
☎ 922 87 11 00
La Gomera's nicely situated *parador* near San Sebastián has a stylish dining room and the best food on the island. Excellent Spanish and international cuisine.

Parador Nacional de las Cañadas (££) Las Cañadas del Teide
☎ 922 38 64 15
The little state-owned hotel-restaurant is unpretentious but correct, offers good food and is the nearest to El Teide and the major volcanic sites.

Restaurante El Sombrerito (£) Calle Santa Catalina, Vilaflor
☎ 922 70 90 52
In Chicho and Ana's simple village restaurant high up towards the Cañadas, enjoy wholesome, authentic Tenerife country cooking. There's a little farm museum and shop attached.

Restaurante Las Rosas (££) Carretera de las Cañadas, La Esperanza
☎ 922 54 84 61
One of the biggest and liveliest authentic eateries in this area southwest of La Laguna, close to the Esperanza forest.

5 Ways to Stay All Winter

EU citizens may work in the Canaries and reside here – though you must apply to the Cabildo Insular, Plaza de España, Santa Cruz ☎ 922 23 95 00

Tout for restaurants The hard-to-find establishments put touts in the street urging passers-by to come and eat. There's a commission on every customer they bring in.

Teach English Locals need English to get on in tourism, but there's a shortage of native English teachers.

Instruct diving/surfing Diving and surfing schools need qualified English-speaking instructors.

Pull pints There's a fast turnover of English- and German-speaking bar staff in all the resorts.

Go to market Toys, jewellery, drawings, sand-art – if you can make anything at all, you can sell it at the markets.

5 Top Beaches

El Médano Tenerife's best natural beaches are the 3km-long pale sands at this small resort.

Los Cristianos The huge 'improved' beaches at this popular south coast resort are the island's biggest and best, especially artificial Playa de Teno, protected by offshore breakwaters.

Playa de las Américas The resort has several good beaches, of artificially improved grey sand.

Playa de Santiago The only notable beach on La Gomera is the long bay of dark pebbles at this sunny southern village.

Playa de las Teresitas Beautiful artificial beach just north of Santa Cruz. Uncrowded on weekdays.

Below: *The sand at Los Cristianos lends itself to sculpture*

EL SAUZAL ✪

29D5
About 16km north of Puerto de la Cruz
Many fish restaurants (£–££)
30 mins from Puerto de la Cruz and La Laguna
Puerto de la Cruz (► 54), La Laguna (► 45)

This community has pretty terraced gardens and attractive homes, as well as an unusual domed church in Moorish style, the Iglesia de San Pedro. Its greatest attraction is the exceptional coastal view, especially from the Mirador de la Garañona, which gazes along the sheer cliffs dropping into the sea. A little further along the road, Tacoronte is the heart of Tenerife's wine-making area, noted for its *malvasia* (malmsey) vineyards and its two handsome, historic churches.

GÜIMAR ✪✪

29D3
About 23km west of Santa Cruz, and 3km inland from the fast coastal highway

Pyramid Park
Calle Chacona
922 51 45 10
Daily 9:30–6
Bars in Güimar (£)
No 120 direct from Santa Cruz every 30 minutes
None
Moderate
El Teide (► 18)
Popular carnival in the first week of Feb, and an ancient midsummer festival in Jun

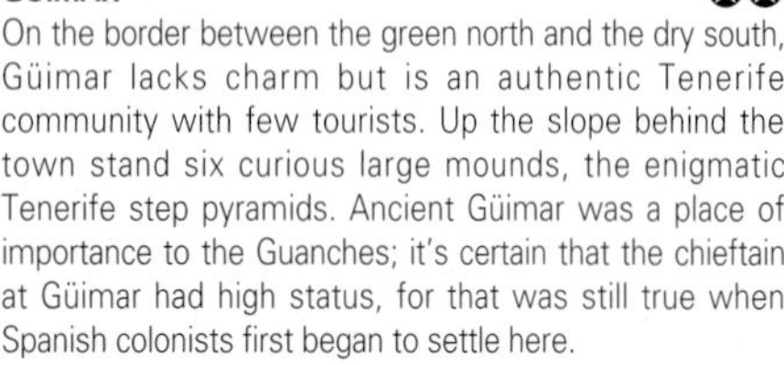

On the border between the green north and the dry south, Güimar lacks charm but is an authentic Tenerife community with few tourists. Up the slope behind the town stand six curious large mounds, the enigmatic Tenerife step pyramids. Ancient Güimar was a place of importance to the Guanches; it's certain that the chieftain at Güimar had high status, for that was still true when Spanish colonists first began to settle here.

First studied in 1990 by Norwegian explorer Thor Heyerdahl, the six geometric mounds were deemed to be no more than piles of volcanic stones cleared from nearby fields by the locals. However, Heyerdahl's excavations showed that the structures are carefully built, arranged in large steps, with a smaller staircase climbing to a ceremonial platform on top. They are aligned with the summer and winter solstices, and closely resemble similar structures in Egypt and Mexico. This not only adds evidence to the theory that the Guanches were Berbers strongly influenced by ancient Egypt, but also suggests the Canaries were part of a prehistoric transatlantic route.

The pyramid area is now enclosed within **Pyramid Park**, with an explanatory visitors' centre, Casa de Chacona. One pyramid has been restored and visitors can decide for themselves what to make of the mystery, which archaeologists are still studying.

Mysterious man-made structures set against the hills at Güimar

Shady Plaza del Adelantado, in La Laguna's historic centre

La Laguna

Outwardly unappealing, the island's second city is a big, sprawling town rapidly spreading towards Santa Cruz, which is only 8km away. Like the capital, La Laguna also has a life and an economy which does not depend upon tourism. Many islanders work here, and there's a thriving university, giving the town a lively, youthful Spanish energy.

La Laguna dates back to 1496, when *conquistador* Alonso Fernández de Lugo set it up as the island's capital, which it remained until 1723. The name means The Lagoon, but there is no lagoon here now (the town is properly known as San Cristóbal de la Laguna). The secret of the town is its exquisite historic quarter, where many fine 16th- and 17th-century Renaissance mansions survive from its earliest days.

It is rewarding to take a leisurely walk around the old centre. To see most of the sights, stroll along Calle Obispo Rey Redondo from Plaza del Adelantado to Iglesia de Nuestra Señora de la Concepción, and back along parallel Calle San Agustín.

DID YOU KNOW?

The Canary Islands are the most westerly part of the European-African land mass, and have always been (and are still today) a last staging post for transatlantic sailors waiting for a good wind before setting off. Thor Heyerdahl's theory, supported by academics and archaeologists, is that the Guanches belonged to a people from the Middle East, who travelled in reed boats to the Canaries and onward from there to South America.

AYUNTAMIENTO (TOWN HALL) ✪

At the start of Calle Obispo Rey Redondo, La Laguna's town hall or *ayuntamiento* is a charming building in Tenerife style. Originally constructed in the 16th century, it was rebuilt in 1822 with fine wooden panelling, and a Moorish-style window. Inside, murals illustrate key events in the island's past, and the flag Alonso Fernández de Lugo placed on Tenerife soil has been displayed here.

Next door, Casa de los Capitanes Generales (House of the Captain Generals) is the impressive residence of the island's military commanders, built in 1624. Today it is used as an exhibition space.

- 29E5
- Calle Obispo Rey Redondo
- Casa de los Capitanes Generales 922 26 10 11

- Mon–Fri 9–1, 4–7
- In Plaza del Adelantado (£)
- Few
- Free

The attractive dome and upper façade of La Laguna's cathedral

DID YOU KNOW?

The end of the eight days of Corpus Christi is just a beginning, for the late May/early June *romería* season then follows, a succession of noisy fiestas and saints days celebrated with passion all over the island.

CALLE SAN AGUSTÍN ✪✪✪

Calle San Agustín
922 25 07 42
In Plaza del Adelantado (£)
None
Free, by appointment

In this delightful old-fashioned street parallel to Obispo Rey Redondo, look out for the Instituto de Canarias Cabrera Pinto (Cabrera Pinto Institute of Canarian Studies), noted for its exquisite traditional patio and handsome bell tower. The fine 17th-century façade next door, of the San Agustín monastery, is an empty shell – the building was destroyed by fire nearly 100 years ago.

CATEDRAL (CATHEDRAL) 

Calle Obispo Rey Redondo
Mon–Sat 8–1, 5–7:30; Sun open for services
Free

The town's large cathedral is much older than it appears, a 19th-century façade covering an edifice which was founded in 1502 but radically modernised during the early 20th century. Nevertheless the dim interior contains a gilded baroque *retablo* (altarpiece), while set back from the high altar is the unostentatious tomb of the island's conqueror and the town's founder, Alonso Fernández de Lugo, buried here in 1525.

IGLESIA CONVENTO SANTA CATALINA (SANTA CATALINA CONVENT CHURCH) 

29E5
Plaza del Adelantado
Mon–Sat 8–12:30, 4–6, Sun 10–12, 4–6
In Plaza del Adelantado (£)
Free

The latticework gallery of the Santa Catalina church, beside the town hall, is one of several attractive architectural features. Inside, the former convent church has a silver-covered altar and baroque *retablos*. Notice the little revolving hatch near the side entrance in Calle Dean Palahi, used by mothers who wished to abandon their newborn girl babies by 'donating' them anonymously to the convent, to be brought up as nuns.

IGLESIA DE NUESTRA SEÑORA DE LA CONCEPCIÓN (➤ 25, TOP TEN)

MUSEO DE LA CIENCIA Y EL COSMOS (MUSEUM OF SCIENCE AND THE COSMOS)

This fascinating and entertaining museum sets out to show the connection between man and the Earth, and between the Earth and the rest of the universe. With a variety of hands-on exhibits and displays, visitors learn about galaxies, our solar system and the human body, complete with such diversions as listening to the sound of a baby in the womb, taking a lie-detector test and watching a skeleton ride a bicycle!

Calle Via Láctea, off the La Cuesta road
922 26 34 54
Tue–Sun 10–8 (shorter hours in winter)
Few
Cheap

MUSEO DE HISTORIA DE TENERIFE (MUSEUM OF TENERIFE HISTORY)

The Casa Lercaro on Calle San Agustín is a grandiose 16th-century colonial mansion, and is the ideal setting for this impressive treasurehouse of island history. The house itself deserves a visit, and anyone really wanting to get a vivid overview of Tenerife's story since the arrival of the Spanish should certainly stop by for a couple of hours at this excellent museum. The collections include historical maps and maritime exhibits, and displays that take the story right up to the present.

22 Calle San Agustín
922 63 01 03
Tue–Sat 10–5, Sun 10–2
Few
Cheap

Below: *exhibits featuring local life in Museo de Historia de Tenerife*

PLAZA DEL ADELANTADO

The heart of old La Laguna is a pleasant, shaded square where locals relax on benches enclosed by some of the most striking historic and dignified civic buildings in town, including the Ayuntamiento (► 45) and the Santa Catalina church (► 46) – as well as beautiful mansions adorned with fine porches and balconies. There are bars here too, and the town's busy Mercado Municipal (main market), with its lattice gallery, is the place to join locals in the morning stocking up with fruit and vegetables.

Mercado Municipal, Plaza del Adelantado
Mon–Sat 8–1
Bars with *tapas* around the square (£)

29F5
North of La Laguna
At Cruz del Carmen viewpoint (££)
Buses operated by Transmersa run into the Anaga Mountains from La Laguna
La Laguna (► 45)

Above: *looking down on Santa Cruz from Las Mercedes in the Anaga Mountains*

LAS MONTAÑAS DE ANAGA (ANAGA MOUNTAINS)

Tenerife's northern range of soaring, wild mountains remains remarkably unspoiled and makes an ideal region for rambling and exploring well off the beaten track. Narrow, twisting roads give access to dramatic landscapes, while for walkers it is still possible to see villages reached only on rough tracks. Here a simple subsistence life continues without any modern conveniences at all. Long-distance paths have been waymarked by ICONA, the Spanish environmental protection agency. The ICONA waymarking is clear, so you're not likely to get lost. However, it is unwise to walk without a map. Walkers' maps can generally be obtained at the Puerto de la Cruz and Santa Cruz tourist offices. The offices may also have information about guided walks in the Anaga Mountains. There is also an information centre at the Mirador Cruz del Carmen, where maps and pamphlets giving details of set walks are available. Part of the region has been designated a protected area, the Parque Rural de Anaga. Yet though impressive and steep, the peaks are not high – Taborno, the highest point, reaches only 1,024m, and a road follows the crests, giving superb views from a string of *miradores* (see panel, ► 93). However, the exposed, northern terrain is often misty, wet or even lightly snow-covered on winter days.

MUSEO ETNOGRÁFICO DE TENERIFE, CASA DE CARTA (► 24, TOP TEN)

NUESTRA SEÑORA DE LA CANDELARIA, CANDELARIA (OUR LADY FO CANDELARIA) ✪✪

The Vergen de la Candelaria, the Virgin of Candelaria, is the patron saint of the Canary Islands and is profoundly revered. She is always depicted holding the child in her right arm and a candle in her left hand. Spiritually, her role is as the symbolic bringer of Christian light to the darkness of Guanche life, and so she represents the rightness and justice of the Spanish occupation of the islands.

The legend told by early Spanish settlers – not by the Guanches – was that over a century before the arrival of the first Spanish *conquistadores* the Guanches found a statue of the Virgin and Child set up in a seaside cave. A multitude of legends claim the statue worked miracles to prevent the Guanches from harming her, and that the overawed Guanches began to worship the figure, which they called *Chaxiraxi*. In a mix of fact and fancy, it is related that the *mencey* (chieftain) of the Guanches welcomed the Spanish at this spot, but that the Guanches were already Christians when the conquerors arrived.

The huge modern (1958) Basilica de Nuestra Señora de la Candelaria, set back from the sea, dominates the village. Inside, the statue of the Virgin sits enthroned in a glorious gilt setting behind the altar, among immense devotional murals. The statue dates from as recently as 1830, and what exactly became of the Guanches' *Chaxiraxi* (which may have looked quite different from today's Vergen) is the stuff of myth. Even before the Spanish arrived in Tenerife, a European living on Fuerteventura is said to have stolen the Guanche statue, but replaced it. Either the original, or its copy, was damaged by fire in 1789 and repaired or replaced. That statue was washed out to sea and completely lost in 1826, being replaced by the present version a few years later. In the big sea-facing plaza outside stand sturdy, dignified, sad statues, representing the Guanche chiefs who were the rulers of the island before the coming of the Spanish.

- 29E3
- On the seashore 17km south of Santa Cruz
- Simple bars in the village of Candelaria (£)
- No 111 (Santa Cruz–Playa de las Américas) stops here every 40 mins
- Few
- Santa Cruz (➤ 32)
- On 14–15 Aug each year the Festival of the Virgin of Candelaria is celebrated throughout the Canaries, and even beyond. Pilgrims make their way to the Basilica at Candelaria for the annual fiesta

The much-venerated statue of the Virgin of Candelaria

PLAYA DE LAS TERESITAS ✪✪✪

29F5
At San Andrés, 8km north of Santa Cruz
Simple bars and restaurants in San Andrés (£–££)
Bus 246 (Santa Cruz–Almaciga) stops here 3–4 times daily
Few
Santa Cruz (► 32)

The delightful beach at Playa de las Teresitas

Despite its huge popularity, the appeal of Tenerife predates the sun, sea and sand recipe of today's mass tourism. Most beaches are unattractive and made of rough, dark volcanic material (which comes as a shock to some visitors). However, island authorities are aware of the lack and have created some artificial beaches. By far the most outstanding of these is the beautiful curve of Teresitas, created in the 1970s with 98,000 cubic metres of sand from the Sahara desert. Ironically, it was created not in the tourist heartland of the south, but in the far north, where locals could enjoy it. San Andrés, at one end of the beach, is a working fishing village.

PUNTA DEL HIDALGO ✪

29E5
20km north of La Laguna
Several bars and restaurants in the resort (£–££)
Bus 105 (Santa Cruz–Punta del Hidalgo) runs every 30 mins
Few
Bajamar (► 41), La Laguna (► 45)

If you want to stay at a Tenerife holiday resort yet get away from it all and remain far from the crowds, come to Punta del Hidalgo. Posed at the end of a small road on the rocky Hidalgo headland projecting into the Atlantic from the northern coast, it is exposed to wild seas and strong winds. The resort does have its following – it's well known as a good place to see the sunset, and its hotels give a fine view over the sea and nearby Anaga Mountains. Most visitors make little use of the sea, preferring to relax at hotel pools. Nevertheless the resort is growing, and gradually becoming a single entity with its similar neighbour Bajamar (► 41).

Northern Hills

Allow a full day to explore the mountainous northern reaches of the island. This is the part which is paradoxically both the most and the least developed, with big working towns on the coast and in the valleys, the simplest hamlets scattered across the upper slopes, and breathtaking panoramic views from the hill crests.

Distance
90km

Time
4 hours

Start/end point
Santa Cruz
29E4

Lunch
There is a restaurant (££) at the Cruz del Carmen mirador

Begin the walk at Santa Cruz, or join at Tacoronte or at any point on the route if coming from the west or south.

Head north for 8km on the coastal highway to San Andrés and the Playa de las Teresitas (➤ 50). Turn inland for 10km on TF112, the twisting, climbing road to El Bailadero.

You're now climbing into the Anaga Mountains (➤ 48). El Bailadero is a magnificent viewpoint, with sweeping vistas of mountain and coast.

Take the high cumbre *(ridge or crest) road, TF1123, towards Mount Taborno. At the fork after 7km, take the summit road.*

A succession of wonderful views along this high road includes the Taborno's spectacular Mirador Pico del Inglés (a few metres up a side turn on the left). Continue along the crest road, with more viewpoints, notably at Cruz del Carmen, where there is a 17th-century chapel and a restaurant.

Far-reaching views from Mirador Pico del Inglés

After Las Mercedes take the right turn at Las Canteras on TF121 to Tejina. At Tejina, follow TF122 as it turns left towards Tacoronte. 7km beyond Tejina, 1km after Valle de Guerra, pause at the Casa de Carta.

The Casa de Carta (➤ 24) is the island's remarkable Ethnographic Museum, housed in a restored 17th-century farmhouse. Continue on this road to Tacoronte, the wine town (➤ 44).

Leave town on the autopista *to return to Santa Cruz.*

The West

If the island is divided into two, north and south, then western Tenerife certainly belongs to the north – it is luxuriant, full of colour, life and history. Yet even so the west is something different. Here, away from the busy valleys and towns of the northern peninsula, there is a sense of space and distance and a remoteness from Spain. The climate is hotter and drier, the land more visibly volcanic, the atmosphere more serene. The dominant feature is El Teide, rising far above all else.

Tenerife's first tourists were drawn to Puerto de la Cruz, and smaller resorts formed to either side of it, clinging to the rocky shores, eventually turning the corner at the Macizo de Teno (Teno Massif) and heading down into the south. Those early holidaymakers belonged to a more refined age, and even today the western resorts retain a calmer, less unruly air and attract a more civilised crowd.

'Doth not a Tenarif or higher Hill
Rise so high like a Rocke, that one might thinke
The floating Moone would shipwracke there and sinke?'

JOHN DONNE
The First Anniversary (1661)

The rock pools (formed by cooling lava) on Garachico's seafront are ideal for swimming

Puerto de la Cruz

28C4
Plaza de la Iglesia
922 36 60 00

Simply 'Puerto' to old hands, Puerto de la Cruz was the first town on Tenerife to attract tourists – and for good reason. Ideally placed for both north and south, close to El Teide, and yet standing at a distance from the workaday world of Santa Cruz, this historic port has a lovely setting. It made a perfect base for the best of leisurely, civilised sight-seeing before the days of 'sun, sea and sand'.

The Port of the Cross (as its name means), built in the 1600s by the settlers at La Orotava, grew into a major port after the eruption which destroyed the harbour at Garachico. Blessed in every way, Puerto is green and luxuriant, with a delightful setting and an exquisite climate. The town clings to the seashore, the lush Orotava Valley rises gently behind and El Teide's soaring peak is clearly visible beyond. Fortunate Puerto is a vibrant, living community which does not depend only on tourism. Its million visitors a year number among the most discerning of the island's tourists, and enhance the town's charming, bustling atmosphere. After the advent of mass tourism, the new crowds were bussed south to purpose-built resorts in the sun, allowing old Puerto to keep its air of dignity. At the same time, it has adapted to the changing needs of tourism, with numerous quality hotels, good shopping, sophisticated entertainment, pretty public spaces and the best family attractions on Tenerife. For dedicated sunbathers, its beautiful lido is one of the most appealing in the Canaries.

Puerto's main church stands among tall palms and flowering shrubs in Plaza de la Iglesia

What to See in Puerto de la Cruz

BANANERA EL GUANCHE ✪✪✪

Bananera El Guanche is a big family entertainment devoted to the subject of the banana – which is, as you will discover, a very strange and interesting plant. Bananera is not only fun and laughter – there's an opportunity to learn here, too. *Bananera* means a banana plantation, and this fruit has become a staple of the island economy (although EU rulings on the minimum size of bananas means that Spain now takes 96% of the island's crop). A video (every 20 mins) explains the process of banana cultivation, which turns out to be extraordinarily complicated and arduous. The banana, we learn, is not a tree, but a bulb, and takes 16–19 months before it produces its first 'hand' of bananas. One of its many oddities is that each plant is both male and female, and reproduces without pollination.

Visitors then stroll along a route which takes them through various kinds of banana plants, as well as many other intriguing species. You'll see varieties as diverse as papaya, mango, the huge and ancient *drago* (or dragon tree) species, sugar cane, cotton, coffee, cocoa, peanuts, pineapples and more. Less familiar names include *guayabero*, kapok and *chirimoya* (custard apples). The cactus garden has hundreds of kinds of cactus, while in the Tropical Plantation there is a wide range of fruit trees as well as datura, tobacco and *chicle* – the South American tree from whose milky resin chewing gum is derived. There are exotic flowers too, including elegant, vivid strelitzia, or bird of paradise flowers, which have become the symbol of the Canaries. Boxed strelitzia flowers are a popular souvenir for Bananera visitors; they can be delivered to your hotel on the day of your flight home.

Finally, before leaving, you're offered a free taste of banana liqueur (powerful – and sweet) and a ripe banana. Many interesting fruit and flower specimens and souvenirs can be bought in the *bananera* shop, carefully prepared and packed for the flight home.

DID YOU KNOW?

The first examples of the banana were brought here some five centuries ago and continued their journey to the newly discovered West Indies. In 1855, a small variety known as Cavendish's Banana or the Chinese Banana was introduced, and became especially associated with the Canary Islands.

28C4
3km from Puerto de la Cruz on the road to La Orotava
922 33 18 53
Daily 9–6
Bar on site (£), restaurants in town (£–£££)
Free bus to Puerto de la Cruz every 20/30 mins daily, 9:30–1, 2–6:30
Few
Moderate

Bananera El Guanche provides an unusual day out for visitors to Puerto de la Cruz

Calle San Juan, off Calle Iriarte
Mon–Sat 9:30–6
None
Moderate

Above: *Casa Iriarte, the birthplace of Tomás de Iriarte, writer of fables and translator of Horace*

CASA IRIARTE

Tomás de Iriarte, born in this house on 18 September 1750, numbers among the very few *Tinerfeños* to have made a name for themselves outside the island. His poetry, plays and essays, and in particular his scholarly translations (for example, from Latin into German), made him a distinguished figure in 18th-century Spanish literary circles. He left the family home at the age of 13 to continue his education in Madrid, where he remained until his death in 1791. This house was once considered an architectural treasure. It has fine traditional carved balconies and a beautiful interior courtyard, still well worth seeing, even though the house is today a charmless souvenir craft shop (one of too many in the area) with a low-key maritime museum upstairs.

Paseo de Luis Lavagi
Ask at tourist office for events and exhibitions
In Calle de San Felipe (£–££)
None
Fee possible
Playa Jardín (► 61)
There are often concerts on Sat evenings

CASTILLO DE SAN FELIPE

A sturdy little beachside fortification, the diminutive Castillo de San Felipe is named after King Philip IV of Spain (1621–65). It was during his reign that settlers began to construct Tenerife's first capital, La Orotava, and its port, Puerto de la Cruz. The Castillo dates from that period, and it remains the best example in the Canary Islands of the Spanish Colonial style of architecture. The building has been immaculately restored and is now a cultural centre. Classical concerts are often given here, which provides the option for visitors of a pleasing change from the usual type of entertainment on offer. The Castillo also houses temporary art exhibitions.

ERMITA SAN TELMO (SAN TELMO HERMITAGE) ✪✪

San Telmo (St Elmo) is the patron saint of sailors, and the seafarers of Puerto de la Cruz erected this simple waterfront chapel in his honour in the 1600s. It's also known as the Capilla de San Telmo (Chapel of St Elmo). Dazzling white but for a tiny bell tower, it is exquisitely pretty, and stands in a lovely little garden surrounded by the noisy ebb and flow of tourists and traffic. Although the street outside is named after the church, as is a nearby beach, there is something that touches the soul in this humble place. Here fishermen gave thanks for having been spared from the dangers of the ocean, while beneath the floor are buried some who were less fortunate, victims of a flood in 1826.

- Calle de San Telmo
- Daily; services Wed, Sat 6:30PM, Sun 9:30, 11AM
- Nearby (£–££)
- Free

The gardens of San Telmo provide a quiet space alongside modern high-rise buildings

IGLESIA DE NUESTRA SEÑORA DE LA PEÑA DE FRANCIA (CHURCH OF OUR LADY OF THE ROCK OF FRANCE) ✪

- Plaza de la Iglesia
- 922 38 00 51
- Daily; service Wed, Sat eve, Sun AM
- Drink or snack on terrace of Hotel Marguesa, Calle Quintana (££)
- Free

Puerto's main church, of dark and pale grey blocks, was started in the 1680s and took nearly 20 years to complete – even then it lacked the pale angular bell tower, added as an afterthought some 200 years later. Standing among the tall palms and flowering shrubs near the elegant central fountain (in the shape of a swan) in the Plaza de la Iglesia, the church possesses a sombre dignity. The baroque interior is decorated with some fine statuary, as well as a good, ornate altarpiece by Luis de la Cruz in a side chapel. The organ comes from London – it was ordered and installed in 1814 by Bernardo de Cologán, one of several Canary Islanders of Irish origin. Notice, too, the amusing pulpit: its wood has been painted to look like marble.

JARDÍN BOTÁNICO (BOTANICAL GARDENS) ✪✪✪

- Calle Retama, off Carretera del Botánico
- 922 38 52 72
- Daily 9–5
- Hotel Botánico (£££); no casual dress
- Along Carretera del Botánico
- None
- Admission charge

One of the most enjoyable places to pass some time in Puerto is the gorgeously, exuberantly lush, exotic and colourful Botanical Gardens on the edge of town. It's the perfect place to rest out of the sun, grab a cool moment of tranquillity, or enjoy a serene park-bench picnic. Here hundreds of intriguing plant varieties grow in profusion, set in a peaceful shady park of only some two and a half hectares. In places, roots, branches and twisting trunks form a fascinating tangle. Almost everything in the gardens is a native of some other land, the focal point being a huge 200-year-old rubber tree, brought here as a sapling from South America. Today it rears up on an astonishing platform of roots. Like the other plants, it has truly flourished in these foreign soils, in an unarguable testimony to the benign climate and conditions of the island.

The gardens were set up in 1788 by King Carlos III as part of an experiment to see if it was possible to acclimatise plants to live in other climate zones. The intention was to see if useful varieties growing in tropical colonies could be 'trained' to survive in the mainland of Spain. The question was reasonable at the time, for it was not known how or why plant species live only in certain parts of the globe. The correct name of the Jardín Botánico to this day is El Jardín de Aclimatación de La Orotava (La Orotava Acclimatisation Garden).

The range of species is prodigious, and includes some 4,000 plant varieties – several of which can also be seen at the Bananera El Guanche (▶ 55). Here pepper trees, breadfruit trees, cinnamon trees and tulip trees mingle with coffee bushes and mango trees. Lovers of exotic

Right and inset: *The Jardín Botánico boasts a wide variety of exotic specimens*

flowers will be thrilled by the splendid hothouse orchids.

Tropical plants that thrived in these gardens were then taken to similar Royal Gardens at Madrid and Aranjuez in Spain to see whether – after their spell of adapting to the climate in Tenerife – they could 'learn' to survive on the mainland. For most, mainland Spain proved simply too cold in winter and the results were broadly unsuccessful. It is now better understood that while some plants can prosper away from home, others can't. For most of the tropical species growing in the Jardín Botánico, Tenerife was as far as they were willing to travel. Many other varieties that were brought here failed to put down roots even in Tenerife.

28C4
Playa Martiánez, Avenida de Colón
922 38 38 52
Daily 10–6
Several eating places on site (£–£££)
Along waterfront
Good
Moderate
Ermita San Telmo (➤ 57)

LIDO DE MARTIÁNEZ (OR LIDO SAN TELMO)

✪✪✪

As a traditional resort, Puerto de la Cruz had a major drawback in the new era of mass package tourism: it had no decent beach. In the 1970s, when the town wondered how to respond to the growing demand for swimming and sunbathing, it consulted César Manrique on Lanzarote. That was an inspired decision. Manrique, an acclaimed international modern artist, had recently returned to his native Canaries, where he had been given a free hand to develop tourist attractions. César Manrique had strong views on mass tourism, which he believed could be of great benefit to the Canary Islands, but at the risk of destroying the landscape and local culture and traditional architecture. He argued that tourism should be encouraged but held within strict controls, and that facilities should be of the highest, most creative standard.

Manrique's solution for Puerto was to create this beautiful lido, completed in 1977 (see also Playa Jardín, (➤ 61), which he developed in 1992). This complex of eight attractively shaped pools and a larger swimming lake, interspersed with refreshing fountains and islets of lush, colourful greenery, has proved a great success. Waterside sunbathing terraces, shaded by palms, are laid out in white and black volcanic rock. Touches of art and humour are

everywhere; a popular feature is a central lava isle which periodically erupts as a fountain. The peak of El Teide can be seen rising inland.

A feature of all César Manrique's sites is that good-quality refreshments are available. At the Lido, several bars and restaurants provide a range of snacks, drinks and complete meals. As at other Manrique sites, the Lido also has evening entertainment aimed at tourists, in the form of the waterside glitzy cabaret 'show restaurant', Andromeda Show Internacional.

Left: *the Lido de Martiánez is deservedly popular with visitors*

LORO PARQUE (➤ 21, TOP TEN)

MUSEO ARQUEOLÓGICO (ARCHAEOLOGICAL MUSEUM) ✪

Located in this interesting area of town near the old fishing harbour, the little archaeological museum is housed in an attractive 19th-century mansion. The emphasis of the museum is Canarian – the culture and ethnography of the Guanche people. The museum hosts a succession of temporary exhibitions. Interesting permanent displays include equipment used in farming, jewellery, weapons and information on mummification of the dead.

- ✉ Plaza del Charco
- ☎ 922 37 14 65
- 🕓 Tue–Sat 10–1, 5–9, Sun 10–1
- 🍴 Inexpensive eating places nearby, especially in Calle San Felipe
- ♿ Few
- 💰 Cheap
- ↔ Plaza del Charco (➤ 62) Puerto Pesquero (➤ 62)

PLAYA JARDÍN ✪✪

After the great success of César Manrique's Lido Martiánez (or Lido San Telmo) further up the Puerto waterfront, the town asked the great Lanzarote artist and designer to see what he could do with the town's grim and gritty black beaches. Manrique chose to landscape the Playa de San Felipe and in 1992 transformed this wave-beaten rocky bay into a remarkable, wonderful waterfront beach garden. The dark sand becomes a dramatically attractive feature, heightened by magnificent gardens of flowering bushes, palms and exotics cultivated on the surrounding sand and rock. Rocks rising inland add to the beauty of the scene. Thousands of offshore concrete wave breakers hidden beneath the water protect Manrique's beach and gardens from the power of the ocean. As a result, Playa Jardín has become a real, popular beach and is now covered with sunbathers.

- ✉ At the western end of town, near Punta Brava
- 🍴 In the nearby fishermen's quarter, especially Calle San Felipe (£–££)
- ♿ Few
- 💰 Free
- ↔ Castillo de San Felipe (➤ 56), Puerto Pesquero (➤ 62)

PLAZA DEL CHARCO

- Off Calle Blanco, near the seashore
- Several bars and restaurants in the square (£–££)
- Puerto Pesquero (see below)

A 'charco' is a lagoon, and this animated raised square stands where once tranquil, shallow waters collected from the sea. Now the plaza, with its ancient Indian laurel tree, is the very heart of Puerto's old quarter and full of life – with bars and cafés, buskers and strollers. The charming restored 18th-century Rincón del Puerto, on the west side, has traditional balconies and an inner courtyard, now occupied by bars.

PUERTO PESQUERO

- At the end of Calle Blanco
- In Calle Blanco and Plaza del Charco (£–££)
- Plaza del Charco (see above)

There's no more picturesque reminder that Puerto does not exist only for tourists than this small working fishing harbour, not far from lively Plaza del Charco. A low harbour wall of black volcanic stone encloses the little bay. Modest but brightly painted rowing boats are hauled up on the shore, where local men and boys gather to talk or work.

On one corner, beside the water, a handsome building of dazzling white paint and bare black stone is the former Casa de la Real Aduana – the Royal Customs House. Built in 1620, this small public office continued to function as a customs house right up until 1833. (It is not open to the public.) Behind are 18th-century harbour defences which protected the town and port from raiders.

Across the street, Casa de Miranda dates from about the same period. It's a fine restored house, once the home of Venezuelan liberator Francisco Miranda, and now a bar and restaurant.

Working fishing boats look decorative and colourful anchored in the harbour at Puerto Pesquero

Around Puerto

Despite the tourist crowds, Puerto retains an atmosphere of grace and history. Much of the central area is pedestrianised, making it enjoyable to walk in the streets of this old colonial town.

Start from the tourist office in Plaza de la Iglesia, a handsome and popular old main square with palms and greenery, a lovely swan fountain, and dominated by the 400-year-old Iglesia (► 58).

Take Calle de Cologán (away from the sea) and turn into the second right, Calle Iriarte.

Reaching Plaza Concejil and Calle San Juan, you'll find the elegant balconied 18th-century house Casa Iriarte (now a souvenir and craft shop and an amateur naval museum, ► 56). Here too is the landmark Palacio Ventosa, with its tall tower.

Distance
1½km

Time
1½ hours

Start point
Plaza de Iglesia

End point
Lido de Martiánez

Lunch
In Plaza del Charco, Calle de San Felipe or at the Lido. *Tapas* bars (£–££) and restaurants (££)

A few paces further on, turn right into Calle Blanco.

This brings you to Plaza del Charco, the pleasantly bustling and shaded heart of town, with bars and shops (► 62).

Take Calle de San Felipe.

Strolling along the waterfront in Calle de San Telmo

This street has unpretentious restaurants and old Canarian buildings of character. Turn right and right again into Calle de Lomo, for the Archaeological Museum (► 61).

Go round the block to return to Plaza del Charco, where you turn left on Calle Blanco towards the sea.

Here is the Puerto Pesquero (► 62), the endearing little harbour with the modest black-and-white Casa de la Real Aduana (Royal Customs House) on one corner.

Walk along the seashore road, known here as Punta del Viento (Windy Point), past a market, and eventually joining Calle Santo Domingo de Zamora and Calle de San Telmo.

Pause to admire the tiny Ermita San Telmo (► 57). Continue to the Lido de Martiánez (► 60).

What to See in the West

- 28A4
- 32km west of Puerto de la Cruz on coast road
- Bars (£) in the main square
- No 363 (Puerto de la Cruz–Buenavista del Norte)
- Garachico (► 20), Icod de los Vinos (► below)
- Fiestas on 17 Jan, 24 Aug, 24 Oct

BUENAVISTA DEL NORTE ✪✪

Buenavista is a pleasant, unassuming little farming town with narrow backstreets and a pretty main square with some 18th-century mansions. The church of Nuestra Señora de los Remedios has fine altarpieces and a notable *mudéjar* (Moslem-style) ceiling. The town's name means Good View of the North, but this small community is 11km from Tenerife's western tip, a headland called Punta de Teno (Teno Point). Good views there certainly are, from Punta de Teno, with its lighthouse and beach, reaching majestically down the cliff-edged coast all the way to Los Gigantes. Half-way to the Punta, the Mirador de Don Pompeyo gives fine views out to sea in the opposite direction. West of Buenavista, the Macizo de Teno (Teno Massif) is one of the most unspoiled parts of the island.

GARACHICO (► 20, TOP TEN)

Walking the dog through the gardens of Plaza de la Constitución in Icod de los Vinos

- 28B4
- 22km west of Puerto de la Cruz on coast road
- Carmen (££), below Plaza de la Iglesia
- Nos 354 and 363 (Puerto de la Cruz–Icod) every 30 mins
- Free
- Garachico (► 20)
- Big fiestas on 22 Jan, 25 Mar, 24 Jun and 29 Nov; festivals of Corpus Christi about 2 Jun, Santa Barbara end Aug and Dragon Tree Festival in Sep

ICOD DE LOS VINOS ✪✪✪

One of the highlights of a tour around Tenerife is the little town of Icod. Its main attraction is the gigantic Dragon Tree known – with poetic licence – as the *Drago Milenario*, the Thousand-Year-Old Dragon Tree (► 17, Top Ten). But Icod has other charms too. The Plaza de la Iglesia, apart from its view of the ancient *drago*, has exotic greenery all around, and a lovely 16th-century church, Iglesia de San Marco. Step inside the church to discover fine altarpieces, a decorated ceiling, and a magnificent 2m-tall cross from Mexico, a masterpiece of delicate silverwork. A welcome escape from the tour bus crowds is to stroll in the nearby streets and squares. As the name makes clear, Icod is also known for its wines. Taste and buy them at the Salón Canario or Casa del Vino in quiet, shaded Plaza del Pilar, or in the excellent Casa del Drago souvenir shop off Plaza de la Iglesia.

LA OROTAVA 

Puerto de la Cruz was originally built as the port for older and grander La Orotava, the hilltown just inland whose coat of arms still declares it to be a Villa Muy Noble y Leal (most noble and loyal town). A jewelbox of balconied façades, pretty decoration, cobbled streets and beautifully preserved historic buildings, La Orotava is best explored on foot. Start with the wonderful views from Plaza de la Constitución. The towers and dome of baroque Iglesia de Nuestra Señora de la Concepción in Plaza Casañas are a distinctive landmark.

Calle San Francisco is the highlight, climbing the west side of town from Plaza San Francisco to Plaza Casañas. Casa de los Balcones (➤ 16, Top Ten) is its main attraction. Across the street **Casa de la Alfombra** (or **Casa del Turista**), though less grand, is half a century older and in the same style, and has a craft shop where demonstrations are given of making sand-pictures, a feature of the town's Corpus Christi celebrations. Also along here, 18th-century Hospital de la Santísima Trinidad used to be a convent – the revolving drum set in the wall by the main door was used to leave unwanted babies to be brought up by the nuns.

Interesting museums in town include **Museo de Artesanía Iberoamericana**, celebrating the artistic and cultural links between Spain (including the Canaries) and Latin America; **Casa Torrehermosa**, showcasing the best of the island's arts and crafts; and out-of-town **Museo de Cerámica**, with 1,000 pieces of traditional pottery. All three are housed in beautifully restored historic buildings.

LOS GIGANTES (➤ 22, TOP TEN)

28C4
5km southeast from Puerto de la Cruz
Modest restaurants and *tapas* bars include Bar Parada (£–££) in Plaza de la Constitución
Nos 345 and 350 (Puerto de la Cruz–La Orotava) every 20–30 mins. No 348 (same route) once daily
Puerto de la Cruz (➤ 54)
Especially noted for its extravagant Corpus Christi celebrations

Casa de la Alfombra (Casa del Turista)
Calle San Francisco
Mon–Fri 9–1:30, 4–7:30, Sat 9–1:30
None
Free

Museo de Artesanía Iberoamericana
34 Calle Tomás Zerolo
922 32 17 46
Mon–Sat 9:30-6
None
Cheap

Casa Torrehermosa
Calle Tomás Zerolo
Mon–Fri 9:30–6:30, Sat 9:30–2
Free

Museo de Cerámica
4km from town centre at Carretera de la Luz – Las Candias
922 33 33 96
Mon–Sat 10–6
No 347 about every 2 hours, 9:10AM–7:10PM
Cheap

Left: *a slightly macabre painted mask in Museo de Artesiana Iberoamericana*
Above: *the impressive façade of the Liceo de Taoro, a private club in La Orotava*

Parque Nacional del Teide (El Teide National Park)

The Guanche name for El Teide, the immense pointed volcano rising at the heart of the island, was 'Tenerife'. For them, the mountain was the island, and in sheer geological terms, that's correct. It was the emergence of this volcano, or its larger predecessors on the same site, which created Tenerife, and subsequently shaped its terrain and dominated its natural and cultural development.

While the northern fringes of the island are fertile and inhabited, the landscape around El Teide remains harsh and unyielding. In particular, the area within the Caldera de las Cañadas, the remnants of a far bigger volcano whose eroded walls enclose El Teide, is an awesome combination of rock and dust. In 1954 the surroundings of El Teide were made a National Park, its boundaries roughly following the borders of the Caldera. Covering 13,500ha, the whole Park is above 2,000m in altitude, and is strictly protected from any development. The Park can be visited by car, by coach (especially on through road C821), or by bike or on foot on numerous smaller tracks and paths. A cable car (*teleférico*) runs up El Tiede to a point 170m below the summit (► 18, Top Ten). The cable car station is 4km from the Parador hotel (► left).

28B3
The park is permanently accessible by road or on foot
Las Cañadas del Teide (££) near the Visitor Centre at El Portillo
No 348 leaves Puerto de la Cruz once daily at 9:15 and arrives at the *parador* at 11:30; return trip at 4. No 342 leaves Playa de las Américas once daily at 9:15 and arrives at El Portillo at 11:45; return trip at 3:15
None
Free
You can stay in the park at the state-owned hotel, the Parador Nacional de las Cañadas (922 38 37 11) on C821 about 4km from the foot of the cable car access point

Above: *the giant crater of Caldera de las Cañadas*

CENTRO DE VISITANTES (VISITOR CENTRE)

The small visitor centre at the high El Portillo pass, east of El Teide on the Park through road, provides a modest and uninspired introduction to the National Park. For walkers, however, detailed maps of the Park are available, and excellent guided walks set out from here (reserve a place by telephoning at least a week in advance). There is no charge, but often the guides do not speak English.

28C3
El Portillo
922 29 01 29
Mon–Fri 9–1:30, 2:30–4
Las Cañadas del Teide (££) nearby
See above
Free

Western Tenerife

This day out takes in all the grandeur of Tenerife's volcanic heartland.

Leave Puerto de la Cruz on the motorway heading towards Santa Cruz, but at Exit 11 (Tacoronte) take C3118 to La Esperanza.

La Esperanza is popular for lunch and a walk in the high pine woods of the Bosque de la Esperanza, just south on C824. This road is the Carretera Dorsal running along the mountainous 'spine' of the island.

Take C824 south from La Esperanza. The road rises through pine woods.

At a bend, a sign points the way to the Las Raices monument, marking the spot where Franco met army officers to plan their coup. Continue to Mirador Pico de las Flores for dramatic views of the north coast. Along the road, pause at other *miradores* – de los Cumbres, El Diabillo and de Ortuño. After 2,000m-high Mirador Ayosa, the road enters the Parque Nacional.

Follow C824 to the junction with C821 and follow it to the left, continuing south.

The Centro de Visitantes (➤ 66), at El Portillo pass, marks the entrance to the Caldera de las Cañadas (➤ 66). After 11km of volcanic terrain you reach the foot of the El Teide cable car (➤ 18, Top Ten) and 4km further, the Parador Nacional, nearly opposite Los Roques de García (➤ 68).

At Boca del Tauce junction, the Cañadas abruptly ends. Return through the park to the Centro de Visitantes.

Beyond the Centro, continue on C821 down into the Valle de la Orotava, passing through heath, vines and, on the lowest level, bananas.

Continue the descent into Puerto de la Cruz.

Below: *Driving along the Cumbre Dorsal road towards El Teide National Park*

Distance
145km

Time
4 hours

Start/end point
Puerto de la Cruz
28C4

Lunch
Las Cañadas del Teide (££)
near the Centro de Visitantes

28C3 / 29E5
Runs from Parque Nacional del Teide to Anaga Mountains

Los Roques de García form part of the extraordinary volcanic landscape

CUMBRE DORSAL ✪✪✪

Of all the routes to El Teide, the most spectacular is the Carretera Dorsal (C824), along the crest of the Cumbre Dorsal – the uplands which run north from El Teide to the Anaga Moutains. Their slopes rise behind the Orotava Valley, with wonderful views to the sides and ahead. Along the road a number of *miradores* make unmissable stopping points. See the Drive on page 67 for more detail.

28C3
Near C821 just south of the Parador Nacional
Book at the *parador* (££) ☎ 922 38 64 15, or Restaurante Boca del Tauce (££) ☎ 922 85 05 2) at the junction with C823
No 348 once daily each way from Puerto de la Cruz terminates at the *parador*. No 342 once daily stops here from Playa de las Américas
Free
Come early to avoid the crowds.

LOS ROQUES DE GARCÍA , LLANO DE UCANCA AND LOS AZULEJOS (GARCÍA'S ROCKS, UCANCA PLAIN AND THE TILES) ✪✪✪

The Roques de García, a cluster of majestic, misshapen columns of rock streaked with colour, are relics of a vanished volcano, a perfect example of the unearthly terrain created by Tenerife's eruptions. The road passes right beside these oddities, which are nearly opposite the Parador Nacional hotel, making it an easy stop. In one direction rises the snow-laced peak of El Teide, while in the other lies the lifeless sandy expanse known as Llano de Ucanca. One kilometre south, make another stop to admire the rocks of Los Azulejos. This geological curiousity takes its odd name – *azulejos* are glazed tiles – from the blue-green mineral glint in the rocks. Such mineral deposits are common in volcanic soils; these are deposits of iron hydrate.

28C3

PAISAJE LUNAR (LUNAR LANDSCAPE) ✪

Accessible only on foot, this area of the Park is a bizarre visual phenomenon. Here, high in the midst of nowhere, strange columns and shapes of tufa rock make a weird unearthly landscape. To reach the Lunar Landscape area involves an 11km round trip on marked footpaths just east of the Parador Nacional hotel.

Walk up El Teide

The ascent of El Teide is *the* walk on Tenerife – though it's actually only suitable for very fit, experienced ramblers. You'll need plenty of water and warm clothes, and should make as early a start as possible, checking with the cable car station that the car is running for the return journey.

Start from the main road C821 at the start of the track to Montaña Blanca.

At first the track passes through a desolate volcanic terrain of sharp, gritty pebbles. After an hour or an hour and a half, you reach the old Montaña Blanca car park.

Follow the sign indicating the Refugio de Altavista, which starts you on a steeper climb on a sandy track. Climb for about 2 hours along this path to reach the Refugio, *or mountain refuge – which may or may not be open (in theory it is open daily from 5PM to 10AM). Continue on the path, the edge of which is clearly marked.*

Some 3 hours later, the path becomes stonier, but more level, passing through a wild, rocky landscape. Eventually you reach the path that leads from the cable car station to the summit. To do this last part you need a permit (► 19).

In a wild, high landscape of multicoloured volcanic rock and scree, the path becomes a steep scramble.

You'll pass sulphurous steam holes emiting heat and vapour from the ground. The views are phenomenal. The summit is marked by a crucifix, where sometimes elderly local women come to say a prayer, seemingly climbing here with ease.

Return to the cable car station and take the car down to the road again.

Distance
8km

Time
6–7 hours

Start point
From C821 Montaña Blanca bus stop
28C3

End point
El Teide cable car station
28C3

Lunch
Take a picnic – no food or water en route. There is a bar (£) at the end of the walk

For an easier walk within the Cañadas region, call in at the Centro de Vistantes (Visitor Centre), on the edge of the park beside the Cumbre Dorsal road (► 66); several good walks start from here. Or take this route to the summit of Montaña Blanca and back

Suitably equipped for their climb, walkers pause to contemplate the rugged countryside

Food & Drink

With so many popular eateries in the resorts focusing on holiday favourites like pizza, pasta and paella, it's easy to forget that most inland restaurants offer traditional local cuisine, usually in cool, simple, tiled surroundings. Look out for the word *tipico*, meaning roughly 'traditional' or 'local'.

Customers at a typical tapas *bar in Puerto de la Cruz*

Fish and Vegetables

Tenerife's staple is quality fresh fish. Most popular are *vieja* (parrot fish) and *merluza* (hake), *abade*, *merro* and *cabrilla* (all forms of sea bass) and *cherne* (a larger bass often cut and served in steaks). Fish is usually prepared in a plain and simple way, such as grilled or fried, and served with a dressing of oil, vinegar and mildly hot peppers or *mojo* (see right) together with a vegetable or two. However, salted fish is also traditional. Among the vegetables, the most typical and traditional are *papas arrugadas,* literally wrinkly potatoes. These delectable salty

Freshly caught local fish displayed for sale

new potatoes, cooked in their skins with plenty of salt until the water has completely boiled away, are properly served with *mojo.* They are a must, and even on their own make a delicious snack.

Stews

The people of Tenerife are fond of hearty stews, usually combining several meats including pork and rabbit with chickpeas and vegetables and often thickened with *gofio* (see below). *Rancho canario* and *puchero* are typical traditional thick meat stews, popular for Sunday lunch. *Potaje*, vegetable stew, is a less meaty alternative (though vegetarians beware, even this might contain a little meat!). The fishy version is *sancocho*, a thick stew of salted fish and vegetables. Served with bread, such stews can make a complete meal.

Multi-coloured produce at a roadside market stall

Gofio

Nothing is more Canarian than *gofio*, the versatile staple of the native Guanche diet that is still very much in use. A rough roasted wholemeal flour (usually of maize, but possibly also of barley, wheat, or even chickpeas), it appears in soups, as a sort of polenta, as a paste mixed with vegetables, or as breads, cakes and puddings.

Mojo

One of the most genuinely Canarian words on the menu is *mojo*. Meat, fish and vegetables may all be served *con mojo*, with mojo, the piquant sauce that comes in different versions, more or less spicy according to what it accompanies. The two main types are *mojo verde*, green mojo, its parsley and coriander recipe giving a cool, sharp flavour, and *mojo rojo*, the spicier, red sauce made with chillis and peppers. Grilled goats' cheese, too, is served *con mojo*.

Desserts

Banana flambé is a must in the resorts, but is not so common in authentic local restaurants. *Gofio* is used to make desserts such as the semolina-like *flan gofio*, or popular *frangollo*, which is made of *gofio* and dried fruit. Syrupy, nutty *bienmesabe* pudding is the Canarians' favourite.

Wine

Tenerife's wines have been drunk in Europe for centuries, traditionally a sweet, rich, heady brew, made from the *malvasia* grape used to make old-fashioned malmsey. Nowadays Tenerife wines can be dry or sweet, red or white. The main wine-growing area is around El Sauzal, just north of Puerto de la Cruz. La Gomera, too, makes drinkable table wine. Make sure you try the sweet dessert wine of Vallehermoso.

Examples of wines produced on Tenerife

BONADEA II
BIG GAME

The South

The climate that caused Spanish colonists to stay in the green north of the island is the very thing that has caused foreign tourists to flock to the south. Everything beyond the volcanic land of El Teide is bone dry, a land stripped bare by Saharan sun. The light is dazzlingly pure and clear, the hills casting magical views across the emptiness to a perfect blue sea. From time immemorial this was the least valuable part of the island, in places little more than a desert. For centuries, up on the slopes some simple, remote shepherd villages survived, while down on the coast the harbour of Los Cristianos benefited from its sheltered position out of the wind. Now, though, the south is full of life and entertainment. Today that once-empty southern coast harvests Tenerife's most valuable crop: sun-seeking tourists. And for them, there can be no better place to be on this island.

'I scarcely ever went out without finding some new wonder to paint, and lived a life of the most perfect peace and happiness.'

MRS OLIVIA STONE
Tenerife (1892)

Puerto Colon marina in the resort of Playa de las Américas

28B1
Exits 27, 28, 29 or 30 from Autopista del Sur
Tourist restaurants (£–£££) near beaches and close to Puerto Colón and Los Cristianos harbour
No 111 to Santa Cruz) Local buses to other south coast resorts; call TITSA in Playa de las Américas 922 79 54 27
Playa de la Troya, Avenida Litoral, Playa de las Américas 922 75 06 33
Few

Los Cristianos and Playa de las Américas

Los Cristianos almost merges with Playa de las Américas; however, it's less brash, more civilised and has a better beach. The throbbing heart of Tenerife's package holiday scene is a round-the-clock resort with a vast choice of accommodation, bars, restaurants and entertainment. Surprisingly, the location is strikingly beautiful, with rocky hills behind. and attractions around the edges of town. The area extends from Los Cristianos in the east, through Playa de las Américas and into the newer district on the west side, Costa Adeje.

What to see in Los Cristianos and Playa de las Américas

San Eugenio Alto, Costa Adeje
922 79 22 66 or 71 52 66
Daily 9–9
On site (£–££)
Free from Los Cristianos
Good
Expensive

AGUAPARK OCTOPUS ✪✪

A hugely popular waterpark (► 107) with pools, rides, slides, flumes, wild water and dolphin displays. Many families, especially those with younger children, prefer to base themselves here throughout their stay.

COSTA ADEJE ✪

Extending west from Playa de las Américas over the area more correctly called Urbanización San Eugenío and incorporating Playa de la Fañabé, this most recent coastal development has set its sights on something more up-market. New hotels here are in elegant neo-classical designs, with masses of marble, pillars, tiles, lush gardens and state-of-the-art facilities. Puerto Colón, the pleasant marina area roughly marking the boundary of the resort, sets the tone with its elegant ocean-going yachts.

Exit 26 off Autopista
922 72 04 03
Daily 10–6
On site (££)
Free
Moderate
Parque Ecológico (► 75)

JARDINES DEL ATLÁNTICO BANANERA ✪

Though a second best to the Bananera attraction in Puerto de la Cruz (► 55), this one offers an opportunity to see, taste and learn about bananas in a genuine banana farm. You'll also learn lots of other things about Tenerife, including its crops and wild plants, and how El Teide distributes the rainwater that falls on the island. Tours round the gardens are accompanied by a guide.

LOS CRISTIANOS 

As this was the only coastal town already in existence in the late 1960s, when sun-seekers first began to head south, it was to this harbour that they came. Los Cristianos already had a few bars and a good natural beach, and owed its existence as a port to a sun-trap location well sheltered from the wind. Even with the subsequent massive growth, the town maintains its separate identity and a refreshing sense of reality which is sometimes lacking at the newer resort next door. The focal point is the bustling harbour area.

PARQUE ECOLÓGICO LAS AGUILAS DEL TEIDE (EAGLES OF TEIDE ECOLOGICAL PARK) 

Here's a lush, tropical park that kids will love as a change from the beach. Not just eagles, but condors, flamingos, pelicans and penguins number among the birdlife living here, while animals include crocodiles, pygmy hippos and elephants. If that's not enough to fill the day, the attractions on site include dodgem boats, a bobsleigh run and other rides.

- On Arona road 3km from Los Cristianos
- 922 75 30 01 or 75 31 61
- Daily 10–6
- On site (££)
- Free bus from resorts
- Few
- Moderate

PLAYA DE LAS AMÉRICAS 

Love it or hate it, you should see it. Look out for the restaurant signs that boast, 'No Spanish food served here!'. One of the most successful purpose-built resorts in the world, Playa de las Américas started construction at the end of the 1960s and has become almost a byword for how *not* to develop tourism. Unfocused, sprawling, much of it frankly ugly, and attracting low-budget packages, it nevertheless rightly remains supremely popular for a fun and sun holiday. Investment in the beach has greatly improved the quality of the sand, the weather is perfect, and there's no doubt that for those who want to start the day with a full English breakfast at lunchtime, swim and tan all afternoon, and disco dance all night, this is the place.

Above: *a panoramic view from Puerto Colón*

Elegant balconies on a late 19th-century building in Adeje

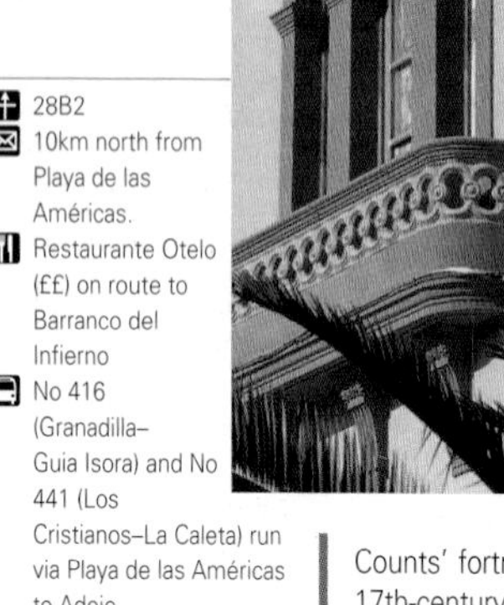

What to See in the South

28B2
10km north from Playa de las Américas.
Restaurante Otelo (££) on route to Barranco del Infierno
No 416 (Granadilla–Guia Isora) and No 441 (Los Cristianos–La Caleta) run via Playa de las Américas to Adeje

ADEJE

One of the few places in the south with a natural water supply, this appealing, unspoiled little southern hilltown is the starting point for walks to the Barranco del Infierno (► 77). Though quite unremarkable now, it was once the seat of an important Guanche *mencey* (chieftain), and then became the Tenerife base of the Counts of Gomera, who had plantations here worked by 1,000 African slaves. Ruins of the Counts' fortress, Casa Fuerte, can be seen, and there's a 17th-century church, Santa Ursula's.

28C1
8km from Exit 26 off Autopista del Sur
Las Galletas waterfront has appealing bars and restaurants (£–££)
No 467 and other buses run between Playa de las Américas and Las Galletas
Few
Los Cristianos (► 75)

COSTA DEL SILENCIO

Its name rather incongruous since the construction here of Reina Sofía airport, this resort zone at the island's southern tip was one of the first to be developed for tourism. There are almost no proper beaches – just the odd shingle strip and a few coves – but several seawater swimming pools make up for the lack. Costa del Silencio includes Las Galletas, a former fishing hamlet with two small beaches and a waterfront promenade, and Ten-Bel, one of Tenerife's first purpose-built resorts.

> **DID YOU KNOW?**
>
> Ten-Bel, on the Costa del Silencio, takes its name from the nationalities of the two business partners who created it in 1969. One was from Tenerife, the other from Belgium.

28C1
22km from Los Cristianos. Take Exit 22 off Autopista del Sur
Bars and restaurants on waterfront (£–££)
No 483 and other buses, Playa de las Américas–El Médano
Few
Los Cristianos (► 75)

EL MÉDANO

A near-constant breeze has been both the blessing and the bane of Tenerife. El Médano, on the island's exposed southeast corner, has its best natural beaches, but is generally too windy for sunbathing to be enjoyable. The solution – this is the island's number one resort for windsurfers. International contests are held here, and anyone who really enjoys the sport should visit. The resort itself, on Punta del Médano (El Médano Point), lacks any charm and is only 3km from the airport. Unspoiled pale beaches extend around bays to both sides and beyond Punta Roja (Roja Point) to the south.

Barranco del Infierno

Together with the El Teide climb, this is one of the two best walks on Tenerife – and much the easier of the two, being on a good path, with no weather problems and no risk of suffering from altitude sickness! Strictly speaking, Barranco del Infierno – Gorge of Hell – is the name of the stream, all the way from its source at over 2,000m, down to the sea. Our walk is in the short stretch above Adeje, where the stream passes through a dramatic canyon, the deepest in the Canary Islands. Wear decent shoes (trainers will do) and start as early in the day as possible to avoid crowds and heat.

Distance
16km

Time
3–4 hours walking

Start/end point
Adeje
28B2

Lunch
Restaurante Otelo (££), Adeje

The well-made path through the Barranco del Infierno gorge is popular with walkers

Start at Adeje (► 76). Take the road that runs uphill through its centre. Continue on the steep road that leads to the gorge path.

At the entrance to the gorge, the path is fairly flat. Notice the caves high in the rock face – Guanche mummies were found in them. The rocky scenery is dramatic. The stream, at first contained in a concrete gulley, is the only permanent watercourse in the south. In places the vegetation is green and lush. Further on, the gorge becomes narrower.

The path crosses and re-crosses the stream, now no longer flowing through a gully.

There are some steep sections, but the total altitude gain is only 300m. Finally the path arrives at La Cascada, a waterfall in three levels pouring into a natural pool, where it is pleasant to rest and swim.

To return, there is no alternative but to follow the same path back.

28C1
3km from Exit 24 off Autopista del Sur
Along Paseo Maritimo (£–££)

LOS ABRIGOS

A fishing village close to the airport, Los Abrigos is noted for a multitude of first-rate little waterfront fish restaurants and has two beaches. Behind the village the Golf del Sur development includes an excellent golf course.

28B2
By Exit 26 off Autopista del Sur
922 79 54 24
Daily 10–7
Restaurant on site (££)
Free shuttle bus from Los Cristianos
Few
Moderate
Costa del Silencio (▶ 76)

PARQUES EXÓTICOS

An astonishing sight in the midst of so much barren terrain, this lush tropical garden east of Los Cristianos is indeed exotic. The main attraction is Amazonia, a slice of tropical rainforest created inside a climatically controlled domed area: it's hot and muggy inside. Parrots, humming-birds and 5,000 butterflies fly around at will. The other section is a Cactus and Animal Park, with a bewildering array of cacti of *all* shapes and sizes! The Animal Park is strictly to amuse the younger ones, with a few friendly caged animals such as marmosets and squirrel-monkeys. What's different is that you can go in the cages.

Parques Exóticos, where rainforest blooms flourish in a tropical microclimate

28C2
On C821, 21km northeast of Los Cristianos
El Sombrerito (££)
No 342 from Playa de las Américas, No 474 from Granadilla and No 482 from Los Cristianos
El Teide (▶ 18, Top Ten)

VILAFLOR

Quite unlike the rest of the south, prettily named 'Flower Town' is the highest village in the Canary Islands. Standing at 1,161m, it rises through cultivated terraces into imposing pine forest on the slopes of the Cañadas, the volcanic El Teide National Park area. The vines of Vilaflor produce drinkable dry white wines, and the village also has an abundant natural spring whose waters are bottled and sold. Although millions pass through Vilaflor on their way to the National Park, few pause here and it remains unspoiled. On the village edge, the Centro de Artesanía Chasno is a good place to buy Tenerife arts and crafts. Just outside the village, set back from C821, the little chapel called Ermita de San Roque stands by the viewpoint Mirador de San Roque. From here, majestic views sweep across southern Tenerife over the areas of cultivation down to the dazzling coast.

A Drive in the South

Leave the resorts behind, climbing into near-barren sun-baked landscapes.

From Los Cristanos take the Arona road, C622 (changes to C822 after the Autopista junction).

Pass through the village of Valle de San Lorenzo to reach Mirador de la Centinela for a sweeping view over a landscape of volcanic cones.

About 2km further on, minor road 5114 turns left towards Vilaflor. It climbs steeply in places, eventually reaching the 5112, where you turn right to continue climbing. The road skirts Montaña del Pozo (1,294m).

Along here walled vineyard terraces climb the slopes to Vilaflor (► 78), the highest village in the Canaries, noted for its white wines.

On reaching Vilaflor, turn left onto the C821 and keep climbing.

Above the village, Mirador de San Roque gives views south. Almost at once the road enters the fragrant pine forest which encircles the Cañadas region. A twisting mountain road through the forest periodically gives good views from *miradores*. El Teide comes into view.

The road leaves the forest and at Boca de Tauce enters the volcanic Caldera de las Cañadas (► 66). Take a left onto the C823 for Chío.

The road cuts across a dark landscape of cones and lava flows. Eventually you reach the pine forests once more. There's a pleasant picnic site and rest area (Chío Zona Recreativa). The road descends sharply. Before Chío there are good views down to the sea, with La Gomera visible across the water.

At Chío junction turn left and left again onto the C822. Pass unspoiled little Guía de Isora. Cross a succession of barrancos *(gorges), eventually reaching the dual carriageway.*

Take Exit 27 for Los Cristianos.

Distance
106km

Time
3 hours driving

Start/end point
Los Cristianos
28B1

Lunch stop
Restaurante El Mirador (££) at Mirador de San Roque, Vilaflor or Las Estrellas (££) just before Chío

The drive passes through the pine forests of Los Retamares, above the village of Vilaflor

La Gomera

Despite its efforts to attract visitors, tiny, circular La Gomera – or simply Gomera – has escaped the onslaught of tourism. A wild green landscape of plunging *barrancos* has made development difficult, just as it made colonisation impossible in centuries past. A new airport in the south may bring more people, but a lack of suitable facilities (though it does have two of the best hotels in the Canaries) ensures that little Gomera appeals mainly to those who need no entertaining, and want only to experience the simplicity and sun-warmed tranquillity of island life. Yet Gomera offers walks, ancient woodland and a dramatic history. The island's capital, San Sebastián, is easily accessible by ferries crossing the 30km from southern Tenerife. Even for those who feel they must be back at their Tenerife hotel in time for dinner, Gomera makes a most memorable day out.

> *'As we were passing, we observed an eruption of the volcano. The smoke and flames, the glowing masses of lava, the muffled roaring from the earth's interior, caused panic among the crew. They believed the volcano had erupted because we had undertaken this voyage.'*

From the log-book of
CHRISTOPHER COLUMBUS,
starting out from La Gomera on his
voyage across the Atlantic (1492)

The yellow-washed church at Vallehermoso

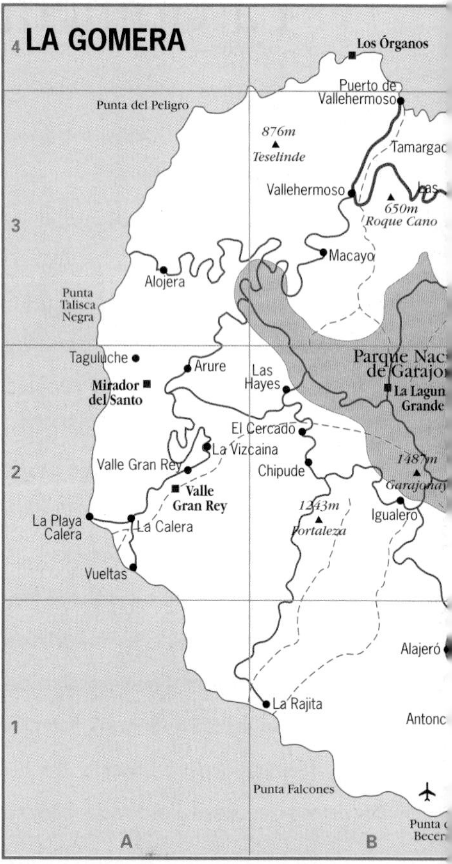

LA GOMERA

4 Los Órganos
Puerto de Vallehermoso
Punta del Peligro
876m Teselinde
Tamargac
Vallehermoso
650m Roque Cano
3
Macayo
Alojera
Punta Talisca Negra
Taguluche
Arure
Las Hayes
Parque Nac de Garajo
Mirador del Santo
La Lagun Grande
El Cercado
La Vizcaina
2 Valle Gran Rey
Chipude
1487m Garajonay
Valle Gran Rey
1243m Fortaleza
Igualero
La Playa Calera
La Calera
Vueltas
Alajeró
La Rajita
1
Antonc
Punta Falcones
Punta Becer
A B

Punta de Agulo
0 2 4 6 km
Agulo
Punta Gabiña
egó de
s Centro
Visitantes
Hermigua
Barranco del Cedro
Las Poyatas
edro
Valle de Hermigua
Punta Majona
Punta Liana
Ermita de NS de Guadalupe
que
del
Cedro
rzita
El Atajo
Degollada de Peraza
Parador Conde de la Gomera
Vagaipala
663m
Roque del Sombrero
SAN SEBASTIÁN DE LA GOMERA
Punta Gorda
Punta Gaviota
Playa de Santiago
C
D

Below: *Playa Calera, a shingle beach beyond the ravine of Valle Gran Rey*

Left: *a goatherd ensures a kid does not stray as she herds her flock along a mountain road*

83C3
25km from San Sebastián on the northern road
Las Rosas (££) in Las Rosas hamlet, 2km west
Hermigua (► 85)
Local fiesta on 25 Apr

AGULO

A pearl of a village in a delightful setting above the coast, Agulo is enclosed by a semicircle of steep green hills, pouring with waterfalls and streams after rain showers. The town's narrow cobbled streets are focused on a domed Moorish-looking church, while out to sea the inspiring vision of El Teide rises from the clouds, above the dark floating form which is Tenerife. It's one of the prettiest spots on the north coast.

82B2
37km west from San Sebastián, off the central highland routes
Four bars (£)
Parque Nacional de Garajonay (► 26, Top Ten)

Above: *above the rooftops of Agulo, the cone of El Teide is seen on the horizon*

CHIPUDE

An undiscovered village that's not so undiscovered any more, Chipude was until recently a simple, rustic hamlet high in the green heart of the island. Among Gomerans its name used to be synonymous with extreme backwardness, ignorance and wretched poverty, and locals will say that the people of Chipude used to drive away intruders with stones. While better roads and communications have changed all that, the villagers preserve old customs and traditions, and it is here that you might hear *el siblo* – not being demonstrated for tourists, but used to call to friends or neighbours (► 99). Chipude has long been noted for its handmade pots made without a potter's wheel and decorated with traditional Guanche symbols, though in fact these are more often from the similar neighbouring village of El Cercado. In the surrounding area are other small, barely accessible rustic villages, including Pavón and Temocodá, also known for their fine handmade pots.

Legend has it that the extraordinary rock formation known as Fortaleza, or the Chipude Fort, 2km south of the village, was a Guanche sacred site. This is easy to believe – its sheer stone soars vertically more than 1,200m to a tabletop crest.

HERMIGUA ✪✪

Lying in the island's most fertile and productive valley, Hermigua threads along the road through its plantations of banana palms. Though one of Gomera's larger towns, it is a tiny, tranquil place. It's a stopping-off point for visitors who want to see local crafts being made and maybe make a purchase at the roomy and interesting Los Telares *artesanía* (craft centre). Nearly opposite is the Convento de Santo Domingo, a 16th-century church with a Moorish-style wooden ceiling.

- 83C3
- 20km from San Sebastián on the northern road
- Restaurante Las Rosas (££ hamlet of in Las Rosas (5km away)
- Agulo (▶ 84)

LOS ÓRGANOS ✪✪

Inaccessible from the land, these strange slender columns of basalt ('The Organs' in English) emerging from the sea to the west of Vallehermoso, are so named because they resemble organ pipes. Extending over a 200m stretch of cliff, and rising to as much as 80m out of the water, the tightly packed hexagonal columns make an impressive sight, and they certainly provide a good excuse for a boat excursion (see right for pick-up points). Surprisingly, they do look just like the pipes of some gigantesque stone church organ.

- 82B4
- 50km from San Sebastián on north coast
- Bars in Vallehermoso (£),
- Only accessible by boat, either from Puerto de Vallehermoso (3km from Los Órganos), or on longer excursions from Playa de Santiago, Valle Gran Rey or San Sebastián
- Vallehermoso (▶ 88)

PARQUE NACIONAL DE GARAJONAY (▶ 26, TOP TEN)

PLAYA DE SANTIAGO ✪✪

In the not-too-distant future, this most southerly point of the island is likely to become the first place to be developed for mass tourism. It already has a handful of bars and tourist restaurants, a waterside promenade and a small stony beach. On a cliff edge above the resort stands the delightful Hotel Tecina, with accommodation in 'cottages' in the beautiful gardens. The new La Gomera airport – initially taking inter-island flights only – is located close by, and the beach is likely to be enlarged and artificially improved. At one end of the Playa the little fishing harbour gives a note of charm. Here a small fishermen's chapel, decorated with model boats, is set into the rock face, as is the restaurant next door.

- 83C1
- 35km southwest from San Sebastián
- Simple places on waterfront (£–££), or, for something special, Hotel Tecina (££)
- Parque Nacional de Garajonay (▶ 26, Top Ten)

An opportunity to watch the process of production of craft items at Los Telares, Hermigua

SAN SEBASTIÁN DE LA GOMERA 

- 83D2
- On east coast of island
- Inexpensive bars in town (£), and the best food on the island at the *parador* (£££)
- The intermittent bus service is not reliable. Taxis are readily available at the ferry dock
- La Gomera Island Tourist Board, 4 Calle Real ☎ 922 14 01 47
- Parque Nacional de Garajonay (► 26, Top Ten)
- Fiestas include the local saint's festival around 20 Jan; Carnaval (Carnival) about the end of Feb; Semana Colombina (Columbus Week) on 1–6 Sep and Vergen de Guadaloupe, 1–6 Oct

Gomera's capital, usually known as San Sebastián and often known to locals simply as Villa, is an unprepossessing little port, though it has an excellent harbour. In several ways San Sebastián is quite untypical of the island. Though hemmed in by hills, the town lies on flat ground, while the rest of Gomera is all steep slopes and valleys; and it stands in a dusty, dry setting though Gomera is largely draped in luxuriating exotic greenery. Most of the town is modern white cubes in an island full of rustic character. Only San Sebastián's picturesque main street, Calle del Medio or Calle Real, and the main square, Plaza Calvo Sotelo, with its balconied mansions, evoke the memory of colonial times and the great drama of the island's history.

The Torre del Conde, built by Herman Peraza the Elder

La Gomera was the last Canary Island to be fully 'conquered' by the Spanish – in fact it remained independent right into the 19th century. As a result, no other Canary Island retains so much of the native Guanche culture and ethnicity. There are, too, visible in many island faces, reminders of the many African slaves who were kept here.

When Christopher Columbus anchored at San Sebastián before the journey that discovered the Americas, this was the most westerly port in the world. Tenerife remained in Guanche hands, while on La Gomera only this edge of the island was under Spanish control.

Pozo de la Aguada (or Pozo de Colón)

- Calle del Medio
- ☎ 922 87 01 55
- Mon–Fri 8:30–2, 4:30–6; weekends 10–12
- The building also houses the tourist office
- None
- Free

To recapture a little of that past, walk along the main street, Calle del Medio or Calle Real. Here is the 17th-century Customs House, or Casa del Pozo, meaning House of the Well. Inside is the **Pozo de la Aguada** (or **Pozo de Colón**), the well from which Columbus's quartermaster drew the water which he was to take to America, and here too the expedition bought seeds, grains and

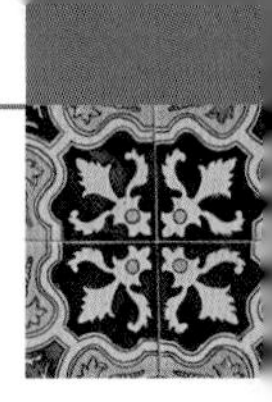

flowers to be planted in the New World. In the same building is the town's tourist office.

In the same street stands **Iglesia de la Asunción**, the 15th-century church, where – we are told, but this is poetic licence – Columbus said his last prayer before setting out on the great voyage. Also in Calle del Medio, **Casa de Colón** (Columbus House) has no proven link with the explorer, but is now claimed as the house where he lodged. It has been restored as a museum about Columbus, featuring models of his ships and old maps, and is the focal point of the town's annual week-long Columbus Festival in September.

Finally, in the harbourside park, the Torre del Conde (Count's Tower, closed to visitors) is the oldest building in continuous use in the Canary Islands. This sturdy brick tower house dates from 1447, and during its most famous era was the residence of the high-handed Countess Beatriz de Bombadilla, wife of the Count of Gomera, Hernán de Peraza. Both the Count and the Countess were hated by Guanches for their repressive arrogance and cruelty. The Count was eventually murdered by Guanches for raping (or seducing) one of their girls, and the Countess moved into this tower for her own protection. It too has a connection with Columbus, for after the murder of the Count, Columbus became friendly with the Countess. Later, fittingly, the tower became a storehouse for gold, silver and treasures looted from American Indians and sent back to Spain.

Iglesia de la Asunción
Calle del Medio
None
Free

Casa de Colón
Calle del Medio
922 87 01 55
Usually Mon–Sat 4–6, but often erratic
None
Free

Brightly painted fishing boats and a larger passenger ship in the harbour at San Sebastián

82A2
52km from San Sebastián
Basic bars and fish restaurants in the beach and harbour area at Vueltas (£)
Occasional buses and boats from San Sebastián
La Gomera Island Tourist Board, Calle Lepanto, La Playa, Valle Gran Rey
922 80 54 58
Chipude (► 84)
6 Jan is the Valle Gran Rey's big fiesta of Los Santos Reyes

Above: *Playa Calera is considered the best beach on the island for swimming*

VALLE GRAN REY

On the west side of the island, the majestic Valley of the Great King was isolated and unknown until the 1990s. Only hippies had heard of it – as a hiding place for an away-from-it-all lifestyle. Today, though, it attracts more visitors than anywhere else on the island, cars and coaches pausing at the lovely Mirador Ermita El Santo at Arure, 10km inland, which shows off the vast, inspiring view of the valley and the sea. From here can be seen the cultivated terraces clinging to the lower slopes of the steep ravine, the scattered white houses of a few hamlets, and the valley opening out to greenery beside the dazzling blue sea.

The village of Arure, behind the viewpoint, is thought to have been the seat of the Guanche chief after whom the valley is named. The road descends the ravine to reach La Calera, the attractive little central community of the Valle Gran Rey, standing among its plantations. Beyond, the road divides for the last 1km to the sea: to the right is the small Playa del Inglés (or La Playa Calera), to the left is the small fishing harbour and port at Vueltas, the traditional gateway to the valley. The shingly little beach is almost the best that La Gomera can offer, and there are simple facilities including waterside eateries offering the freshest of fish.

82B3
In northwest, at junction of TF711 and TF712
Two bars with *tapas* in the village centre (£)
Los Órganos (► 85)

VALLEHERMOSO

An attractive and appealing village – one of the island's largest communities – Vallehermoso is indeed in a 'Beautiful Valley' as its name suggests. It is surrounded by forest, vineyards and palm plantations of date and banana. A striking 650m-high pinnacle of volcanic rock close by is called Roque Cano, Dog Rock, supposedly for its resemblance to a dog's tooth.

Northern Gomera

The deeply cut, forested terrain defies land travel, and until recently most journeys were made by boat, around the perimeter of the island.

Distance
50km

Time
2–3 hours

Start point
San Sebastián de la Gomera
83D2

End point
Puerto de Vallehermoso
82B4

Lunch
Restaurant Las Rosas (£)

Start out from San Sebastián on the Hermigua road, TF711.

The road climbs steeply up the Barranco del Cedro, giving views over the water to Tenerife, and passes by the large statue of Jesus which overlooks San Sebastián.

The road climbs higher and crosses into the National Park area.

Here the road winds through unspoiled dense mixed woodland of laurel, beech, pine and flowering heather trees, even though the name at this point is Bosque del Cedro (Forest of the Cedar).

After sharp turns and a tunnel, the road begins descending towards the north coast.

Wonderful views contrast green valleys and the dazzling blue ocean as the road descends into Hermigua (► 85) and, 2km further, Agulo (► 84).

The road, winding all the time, climbs inland beside a plunging green valley, passing Las Rosas restaurant and continuing to Vallehermoso.

At Tamargada, pause at a fine *mirador* to look at the forest. At Vallehermoso (► 88) there is abundant cultivation of date palms and bananas. Many date trees have been cut and have metal cups attached to gather the sap for Gomera's speciality, Miel de Palma, a syrup made from date sap.

The tree-covered hillsides beyond Vallehermoso

A very poor road, the TF712, leads down to the shore at Puerto and Playa de Vallehermoso.

From Puerto, regular boat trips go out to see the strange rock formations of Los Órganos (► 85).

Where To...

Above: *enamelled brooches on a pavement stall*
Right: *a shop sign in La Laguna*
Left: *Playa Jardín, Puerto de la Cruz*

The North

Prices
Approximate price of a three-course meal for one, without drinks.
£ = under 2,000 ptas
££ = 2,000–3,000 ptas
£££ = over 3,000 ptas

Norwegian Connection
The Pyramid Park at Güimar, on the east coast, first proposed by Norwegian explorer and anthropologist Thor Heyerdahl, has been funded by shipping magnate Fred Olsen, a fellow Norwegian. There's more about the Tenerife pyramids on the FERCO website, www.ferco.org.

Bajamar

Café Melita (££)
More of a café and cake shop than a restaurant, this German-run place in the little north coast resort specialises in desserts, pastries and rich cakes. Lovely sea views.
✉ Punta del Hidalgo, 3km north ☎ 922 54 08 14 ⌚ Lunch 🚌 No 105 (Santa Cruz–Punta Hidalgo) half-hourly

Candelaria

Sobre El Archete (££)
There's high-quality creative Canarian cooking at this smarter-than-usual restaurant, something of a find in this part of the island. It makes a pleasant lunch spot after seeing the church in the little pilgrimage town.
✉ 2 Lomo de Aroba
☎ 922 50 01 15 ⌚ Lunch

El Sauzal

Casa del Vino (££)
The interesting wine museum and wine-tasting centre in El Sauzal also has a good, busy restaurant, which for some is the main reason to visit. The outdoor terrace has sea views.
✉ La Baranda ☎ 922 56 33 88 ⌚ Tue–Sun 11–8

El Calvario (££)
This very unassuming-looking cavernous roadside bar-restaurant is an excellent spot for typical Canarian cuisine, especially traditional meat dishes. Order a local wine to go with them.
✉ On C820, near Tacoronte
⌚ Lunch, dinner

La Cabaña (££)
On the road from Tacoronte to El Sauzal, this is one of several good eating places. Unpretentious and down to earth, with green and white exterior and a Coca Cola sign outside, it specialises in Argentinian-style meat dishes.
✉ On C820, near Tacoronte
⌚ Lunch, dinner

La Esperanza

Restaurante Las Cañadas (££)
Coloured lights and Canarian-style balconies set the tone for this restaurant, popular with locals. It's one of several jolly eating houses in this farming area attracting groups and families for traditional roast meats, local wine and plenty of loud talk and laughter.
✉ 71 General de la Esperanza
☎ 922 54 80 30
⌚ Lunch, dinner

Restaurante Las Rosas (££)
Of the big, lively eateries that draw locals and tourists alike to feast and have fun in this area southwest of La Laguna, this is one of the biggest and liveliest. Herby roast meats, salads, inexpensive wines.
✉ Carretera de las Cañadas
☎ 922 54 84 61
⌚ Lunch, dinner

La Laguna

Casa Maquila (£)
La Laguna is not a place for fine dining, though there are some good restaurants out of town. While sightseeing in the centre, you should choose a typical *tapas* bar, and settle down to local specialities, properly prepared – at somewhere like this simple and agreeable restaurant.
✉ Callejón Maquila 4
☎ 922 25 70 20
⌚ Lunch, dinner

Hoya del Camello (££)
It's a short distance out of town, but this moderately priced establishment is one of the La Laguna area's better restaurants, with a good range of well-prepared international, Spanish and Canarian favourites.
✉ 118 Carretera General del Norte, San Lazaro ☎ 922 26 20 54 🕐 Lunch, dinner

Los Naranjeros

Los Limoneros (££)
This rural but very civilised spot off the motorway near La Laguna draws local families for big, well-prepared dinners and weekend feasts of international and local specialities, including rabbit in spicy sauce, and lamb and goat dishes. Service is good.
✉ Los Naranjeros, 4km east of Tacoronte ☎ 922 63 66 37 🕐 Lunch, dinner

San Andrés

The cluster of humble fish restaurants (£–££) along the waterfront of this little harbour village is well known to locals. All the restaurants serve seafood and the fresh catch of the day, at similar prices. Just beyond is Playa de las Teresitas, the island's most beautiful beach.

Santa Cruz

Café del Príncipe (£–££)
Attractive and authentic place well situated in one of the most appealing squares in Santa Cruz. Sit out with locals and tourists and enjoy a drink, a snack or a complete meal of typical island specialities.
✉ Plaza del Príncipe de Asturias ☎ 922 27 88 10 🕐 All day

El Coto de Antonio (£££)
Rambla del General Franco curves round the city centre. Along here, and northwest of the road, there are several smart, pricey eating places catering not especially for tourists but mainly for business people and well-to-do locals. This is a top example, serving good fresh cooking from seasonal ingredients.
✉ 13 Calle General Goded ☎ 922 27 21 05 🕐 Lunch, dinner 🚌 Frequent town buses along the Rambla

Los Troncos (££)
Among the very best restaurants in the Tenerife capital, in the smart northwest area, and yet surprisingly inexpensive. Noted for Canarian cooking of a high standard, and also for Basque specialities.
✉ 17 Calle General Goded ☎ 922 28 41 52 🕐 Closed Wed, Sun pm, and mid-Aug to mid-Sep 🚌 Frequent town buses along the Rambla

Olympo (£)
This popular bar-restaurant may be touristy, but locals gather here also to enjoy a drink or a meal in a pleasant setting in the heart of town. Good set lunch at a moderate price.
✉ Plaza de Candelaria ☎ 922 24 17 38 🕐 All day

Parque Marítimo César Manrique (£–£££)
It was part of César Manrique's philosophy that all tourist attractions should offer good eating and drinking facilities on site. His Lido on the Santa Cruz waterfront does visitors proud, with a range of eating from the Cafeteria Central and self-service Buffet to the Restaurante Cascada and Restaurante Aría.
✉ Castillo de San Juan, off Avenida de José Antonio Primo de Rivera, 1km south of Plaza de España ☎ 922 20 32 44 🕐 Daily 10–6 🚌 Frequent town buses along Avenida de José Antonio Primo de Rivera

Anaga Views
Most accessible of the Anaga viewpoints is Mirador de Jardina, near La Laguna. Much higher is Mirador Cruz del Carmen (920m), which gives a view of both coasts. Here stands a lonely 17th-century chapel, the Ermita Cruz del Carmen. Alongside there is a restaurant, and an information centre on the Parque Rural de Anaga. A short distance further along the road, on the slope of Taborno, Mirador Pico del Inglés (992m) is the highest viewpoint. Nearer the northern tip of the range, Mirador Taganana gives a lofty view onto the sugar-cube village of Taganana.

The West

Canary Wine
'But that which most takes my Muse, and me, is a pure cup of Canary Wine.'
– Ben Jonson, Elizabethan playwright

Canaries – Islands, Birds ... and Dogs
It is sometimes thought that the Canaries are named after the canary, a yellow cage bird seen all over the world. The bird is a Canary Islands native, and common in western Tenerife – although the wild native has a less yellow plumage than the cage variety. However, the bird is named after the islands rather than the other way round. The Canary Islands were so named for their wild dogs (*canes* in Latin), that had been observed by early visitors on the island of Fuerteventura.

Garachico

Bodegón Plaza (£)
Enjoy dining in a homely, domestic setting where simple and tasty traditional local cooking is served in several rooms. Very reasonable prices.
Calle Estaban de Ponte 922 83 09 77 Lunch, dinner No 363 (Puerto–Buenavista) hourly

Isla Baja (££)
Respected due to its long-standing reputation, this rather pricey restaurant is located on the waterfront facing the Castillo de San Miguel. It specialises in good local fish dishes, though you can also stop by just for a drink, snack or ice-cream.
Calle Estaban de Ponte 922 83 00 08 Lunch, dinner No 363 (Puerto–Buenavista) hourly

Icod de los Vinos

Carmen (££)
Considered the best place to relax, get away from the coach parties, and tuck in to some traditional Spanish cooking before or after peering at the giant Dragon Tree, nearby.
Below Plaza de la Iglesia 922 81 06 31 Lunch, dinner Nos 354 and 363 (Puerto–Icod) both hourly

Restaurante Plaza la Pila (£)
Here tasty local dishes are cooked without fuss and served in a simple setting.
Plaza la Pila 922 82 27 02 Lunch, dinner Nos 354 and 363 (Puerto–Icod) both hourly

La Orotava

Casa Gabriel (££)
In a town with few eating places to tempt the tourist, here's somewhere down-to-earth to relax and enjoy good unpretentious Spanish food at modest prices.
5 Camino de los Rechazos
922 33 55 91
Lunch, dinner

Los Gigantes/Puerto de Santiago

Casa Pancho (££)
This authentic restaurant comes as a surprise in a popular little sun-and-sea resort area, catering mainly to British people on package hols and with few signs of any indigenous local life. A genuine Spanish restaurant serving Spanish food to a high standard – there's nowhere else quite as good for miles.
Playa de la Arena 922 10 13 23 Lunch, dinner No 473 (Los Gigantes–Las Galletas, south of Los Cristianos)

Masca

Casa Enrique (£)
This off-the-beaten-track village in the Macizo de Teno has become a popular coach stop, where visitors can get a glimpse of the simple Canarian life. The unpretentious bar-restaurant offers traditional tasty Canarian vegetable stews, *gofio*, local fried goats' cheese and traditional desserts – all at low prices.
Masca centre Lunch

Parque Nacional

(including perimeter outside boundary of Park)
Restaurante Boca del Tauce (££)
This restaurant stands in the volcano region at the junction of the Park's

through road C821 and the highway on its southwestern flank C823. It's an excellent, friendly place to enjoy a meal of Canarian or international dishes, with good service.
Boca del Tauce junction, on Chío road 922 85 05 29 Lunch No 343 (Playa de las Américas–Las Cañadas) once daily meets No 348 (Puerto–Las Cañadas) once daily

Restaurante Las Estrellas (££)
Out of the crossroads village of Chío, on the southwest side of the Park boundary, this bar-restaurant enjoys stirring views reaching over the coasts.
Chío All day No 460 (Icod–Guía de Isora, via Chío) every 2–3 hours

Parador Nacional de las Cañadas (££)
The little state-owned *parador* is high in the Park and close to El Teide and all the major volcanic sites. The restaurant is unpretentious but correct, offers good food and is open to the public.
Las Cañadas del Teide 922 38 64 15 Lunch, dinner No 343 (Playa de las Américas–Las Cañadas) once daily meets No 348 (Puerto–Las Cañadas) once daily

Puerto de la Cruz

Buccaneer (££)
An old favourite among British expatriates and regular visitors, this pub-style restaurant offers karaoke, parties and quizzes, carvery-type eating and 'The Best Sunday Lunch in the North'.
Calle La Hoya Lunch, dinner

Casino Taoro (£££)
Puerto's casino is in Parque Taoro, the park set back from, and above, the bustle of the town. The casino restaurant attracts a dressed-up crowd and caters for them in style, with red-draped tables, formal service, smart atmosphere and a predictable range of classy international dishes. Good views.
Casino, Parque Taoro 922 38 05 50 Dinner

La Casona (££)
Cook your own steak on a slab of hot stone at La Casona, one of the best of several Canarian-international eating choices in Rincón del Puerto, a handsome historic mansion and courtyard in Puerto's main square.
13–14 Plaza del Charco 922 38 19 52 Lunch, dinner

La Parilla (£££)
This smart restaurant is located in one of Tenerife's most luxurious hotels, the Botánico, but is open to the public. It offers top of the range international and French-style cooking, and slick service in an elegant setting. You may feel out of place if you are dressed too casually.
Hotel Botánico, Avenida Yeoward 922 31 14 00 Dinner

Lido de Martiánez (£–£££)
Several quality bars and restaurants provide a range of snacks, drinks and complete meals in this attractive lake and pool complex (► 60).
Playa Martiánez 922 38 38 52 Daily 10–5, then Andromeda open in evenings until late

African Wind
Claims that Tenerife's climate is 'perpetual spring' are belied by periods of sirocco. This hot, dry, dusty wind blows straight off the Sahara desert for days at a time, usually in spring and autumn. Temperatures rise to as much as 45°C, and the weather is known to locals as El Tiempo de África (African time).

Be Polite
You'll notice that locals entering or leaving a restaurant often address the room at large with a quiet greeting of 'Señores, señoras'. This is simple politeness. When speaking to Spaniards, a formal use of titles is considered normal, and makes a good impression even if your Spanish is not very good. Address men as Señor, women as Señora, and young unmarried women as Señorita.

Magnolia (£££)
Top-class dining, indoors or al fresco, at this award-winning restaurant attracts discerning locals and well-to-do Spanish visitors. Food is a mix of Catalan and international, with an emphasis on fish and seafood. You'll find the restaurant out of town in the La Paz urbanización.
Carretera del Botánico 5, Avenida del Marqués de Villanueva del Prado
922 38 56 14 **Dinner**

Mario (£–££)
One of the choice of eating establishments in the fine old Rincón de Puerto building, this one specialising skilfully in fish dishes. If you just want *tapas*, pop into adjacent Olympia.
13–14 Plaza del Charco
922 38 55 35
Lunch, dinner

Mi Vaca y Yo (££)
It looks down to earth and rustic, but this restaurant near the fishing harbour is one of the best in town for exceptional fish and seafood dishes. There are lots of traditional Canarian dishes on the menu, but also a choice of Spanish and international favourites.
3 Calle Cruz Verde
922 38 52 47 **Dinner**

Régulo (££)
Popular, atmospheric and attractive with its plants and patio, this is an agreeable example of the many good little fish restaurants near the fishing harbour, in the fishermen's quarter near Plaza del Charco.
16 Calle San Felipe
922 38 45 06 **Lunch, dinner. Closed Sun and Jul**

Restaurante La Cuadra (£)
A popular venue where ocals join visitors to drink, enjoy a typical *tapas* snack, or sit down to a hearty well-prepared Spanish meal at tables set out on the main street leading down to Plaza del Charco.
Junction Calle Blanco and Calle Iriarte **922 38 02 71**
Lunch, dinner

Restaurante Plaza la Pila (£)
At this agreeable and unpretentious restaurant, tasty local dishes are cooked without fuss and served in a simple setting.
Plaza la Pila
922 82 27 02 **Lunch, dinner**

Santa Ursula

El Lagar (££)
Locals and long-stay Tenerife fans leave Puerto and come to the Santa Ursula eateries (such as this one for traditional meat, vegetable and fish stews, and chicken, pork and beef dishes. The proprietors of this one place more emphasis on international styles of cooking.
85 Cuesta de la Villa **922 30 06 55** **Lunch, dinner**

Los Corales (££)
In the Santa Ursula area, about 10km north of Puerto, several good little restaurants like this specialise in typical Canarian fish stews, and fried eel, as well as a range of more familiar dishes. Local wines are served.to accompany the food.
42 Cuesta de la Villa
922 31 02 49
Lunch, dinner

The South & La Gomera

Adeje

Restaurante Otelo (££)
Get a drink or a decent meal at this modest, likeable bar-restaurant brilliantly situated near the entrance to the Barranco del Infierno. Well known to the expatriates and old Tenerife hands, it's especially popular for the island's traditional rabbit dishes, spicy chicken and Canarian specialities. Hearty portions and a pleasant atmosphere.
✉ Barranco del Infierno ☎ 922 78 03 74 ⊕ All day. Closed Tue

Los Abrigos

La Lagostera (£–££)
Drive past the new Golf del Sur developments and down to the sea. This is just one of a cluster of tempting little fish restaurants at this tiny waterside harbour along the Costa Silencio. Here the fish is sold by weight: enjoy the freshest and simplest of Canarian cooking, with some good inexpensive wine.
✉ Paseo Maritimo ☎ 922 17 03 02 ⊕ Lunch, dinner

Los Cristianos

The resort has scores of tourist-oriented eating places, with more of them reaching a high standard of service and cuisine than is the case in neighbouring Playa de las Américas.

Casa del Mar (££)
On a corner of the busy Los Cristianos harbour, this upstairs restaurant offers a good view over the port's activities, and serves a choice of Canarian, Spanish and international favourites.
✉ Harbour ☎ 922 79 32 75 ⊕ Lunch, dinner

El Alazan (££)
This bar in the El Cabezo area specialises in *areperas* – small snacky dishes from Venezuela, made of fried flour and filled with a variety of meat or fish, and sometimes served with a spicy *mojo*–style sauce.
✉ Calle San Roque ⊕ All day

El Bote (£)
A likeable little bar, with plenty of character. The bar itself is ingeniously set inside a rowing boat! This is a good place to come for *tapas*.
✉ Calle El Cabezo ⊕ All day

El Sol (£££)
This place has a well-deserved reputation for Canarian and international cooking, stylishly served, though you do have to pay fairly high prices for the privilege.
✉ Calle El Cabezo ☎ 922 70 05 69 ⊕ Lunch, dinner

La Cava (££)
A breath of fresh air after a surfeit of touristy eating places, this establishment provides a chance to enjoy authentic Spanish cooking in a pleasant outdoor ambience.
✉ Calle El Cabezo ☎ 922 79 04 93 ⊕ Lunch, dinner

Rincón del Canario (££)
Here's a bright and amiable place to enjoy authentic local fish dishes in a simple setting. A fishing boat outside sets the tone of the restaurant. Service is relaxed – maybe too relaxed!
✉ Calle El Cabezo ☎ 922 79 56 14 ⊕ Lunch, dinner. Closed Mon

Trade Winds
On Tenerife and La Gomera, the northerly trade winds – known as los Alisios – bring settled weather of rainfree days with some cloud. On the north or west of the islands, the wind can be troublesome, and cloud cover excessive. In the south, it means perfect holiday weather.

Little Italy
If you'd rather eat good-quality Italian food than search out Spanish in the heart of the big resorts, life will be easy. The Little Italy chain has nine good restaurants in Playa de las Américas and Los Cristianos – all with Little Italy in their name.

Swiss Chalet (££)
You'll eat plenty of Italian food in Tenerife, as well as – it is hoped – Spanish and Canarian, but for a change here's something completely different and surprising. This place specialises in delicious fondue, the melted cheese dish more usually associated with ski resorts.
✉ Avenida de Suecia ☎ 922 79 14 26 ⏲ Lunch, dinner

Playa de las Américas/Costa Adeje

There are literally hundreds of almost identical restaurants along the coast road through the resort. Their basic meals of pasta, pizza, paella, steak or fish and chips, and other international favourites, are displayed in photos on boards outside.

Ambassadeur (££)
A rare example of a dinner-dance venue offering high-quality international fare. There's a cocktail bar, live music and a spacious dance floor. Open till the early hours, but they stop serving meals at midnight.
✉ Starco Commercial Centre, Avenida Litoral ☎ 922 75 16 65 ⏲ Dinner. Closed Sun

El Dornajo (££)
It's still possible to eat like a local in Playa de las Americas, at this enjoyable and genuine grill restaurant near the sea.
✉ Avenida Litoral ☎ 922 79 14 25 ⏲ Lunch, dinner

El Patio (£££)
Among the very best dining experiences on the south coast is a meal on the terrace of this excellent hotel-restaurant near the Puerto Colón, where Playa de la Américas meets Costa Adeje. The cooking is high-quality Canarian and mainland Spanish.
✉ Jardín Tropical Hotel, Calle Gran Bretaña, Urbanización San Eugenío ☎ 922 79 41 11 (ask for restaurant El Patio) ⏲ Lunch, dinner

Mamma Rosa (£££)
This very popular restaurant demands a certain smartness from diners to match the good food, fine wine and professional service. Despite the name, the food is not exclusively Italian.
✉ Apartamentos Colón II, Avenida Litoral ☎ 922 79 48 19 ⏲ Lunch, dinner

Poris de Abona

Los Burros Alegres (££)
Along the barren southeast coast are scattered beaches and small communities, Poris de Abona being one of the largest, and a stop on the bus route. This is not a restaurant, but a riding school, also offering donkey and camel rides, with lunch included. It offers popular barbecue-style eating, though the main speciality is fresh fish.
✉ Maretas del Rio ⏲ Lunch 🚌 No 111 (Playa de las Américas–Santa Cruz) stops here every 40 mins

San Isidro

Bodega El Jable (££)
In this untouristy inland village near the motorway, close to the El Médano exit, there's an appealing and popular bar-restaurant serving hearty Canarian cooking.
✉ 9 Calle Bentejui ☎ 922 39 06 98 ⏲ 1–4, 7:30–11. Closed Sun and Mon lunch 🚌 No 111 (Playa de las Américas–Santa Cruz)

Vilaflor

Restaurante El Mirador (£–££)

The name tells you everything – this restaurant bar stands just off the road below Mirador de San Roque, by the little Ermitage de San Roque. Enjoy outstanding views and good Canarian cooking.

On C821, Ermita de San Roque Lunch No 342 daily from Playa de las Américas, No 482 from Los Cristianos and No 474 from Granadilla

Restaurante El Sombrerito (£–££)

The village restaurant of El Sombrerito belongs to Casa Chicho, the family-run inn (➤ 104). In Chicho and Ana's simple, friendly restaurant, you can enjoy wholesome Canarian meals using authentic Tenerife country recipes. There's a little farm museum and shop attached.

Calle Santa Catalina 922 70 90 52 Lunch, dinner No 342 daily from Playa de las Américas, No 482 from Los Cristianos, and No 474 from Granadilla

La Gomera

El Pajar (£)

Where do islanders go for a drink or meal? Drop in to this cheerful, animated bar-restaurant to get a glimpse into the life of the locals. Good no-nonsense Spanish cooking.

44 Calle Ruiz de Padrón, San Sebastián 922 87 11 02 All day

Hotel Jardín Tecina Restaurant (££)

The terrace of this excellent hotel on La Gomera's south coast offers international dining and a wonderful view of the sea.

Lomada de Tecina, Playa de Santiago 922 14 58 50 Lunch, dinner

Las Rosas (££)

Not just a place to eat, this pretty roadside restaurant is an essential stopover on a tour of La Gomera. Its superb valley-edge location and views and, most of all, its fascinating demonstrations of *el siblo*, the island's unique whistling language, attract coach parties every day. This may be your only opportunity to hear this dying form of communication (➤ panel, right), so that is a sufficient reason to come. However, the food and setting are delightful too, with typical well-prepared Canarian specialities.

Las Rosas 922 80 09 16 Lunch only. Book ahead

Marqués de Oristano (££)

If you're in San Sebastián, this is the place to try for a decent lunch or dinner before or after the ferry. It has a pleasing atmosphere and attractive terrace.

24 Calle del Medio, San Sebastián 922 87 00 22 All day

Parador de San Sebastián de la Gomera (££–£££)

Gomera's state-owned *parador* has an excellent restaurant with a fine location, stylish dark-wood dining room, and the best food on the island. Spanish and international cuisine. (➤ 104, Where to Stay, for more about the *parador*.)

Balcón de la Villa y Puerto, Lomo de la Horca 922 87 11 00 Lunch, dinner

El Siblo

Of all the distinctive elements in Canarian culture, few are more astonishing than the 'whistling language' of La Gomera. In response to similar conditions that gave rise to yodelling in Switzerland – needing to communicate across steep terrain and dense forests – the Gomerans developed a whole vocabulary, syntax and grammar of whistles. Another quality of *el siblo* is its volume: skilled *silbadores* can whistle a detailed message to another person several miles away.

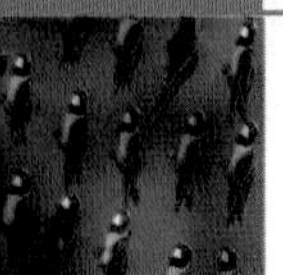

The North

For a double room in mid-season expect to pay
£ = under 10,000 ptas
££ = 10,000–20,000 ptas
£££ = over 20,000 ptas

On the Cards
Credit cards are widely accepted in both large and small shops in Santa Cruz, Puerto de la Cruz and the Playa de las Américas area. In other towns, and all over La Gomera, expect to be told only cash is acceptable.

Timeshare Dreams
Tenerife is timeshare land, where touts pester, lure and tempt the unwary into signing away their savings in exchange for a-week-a-year at a resort apartment block. Lavish inducements are given, not just to sign, but even to see the property. Timeshare is not a bad idea – you don't have to use your annual week or two weeks; you can rent them out, or swap them for a fortnight in Florida or Florence. Don't agree to pay anything without legal advice, and be sure you are informed about Spanish property law and taxes.

Candelaria

Tenerife Tour (££)
Moderately sized (173 beds), this reliable three-star low-rise hotel, with pool and tennis courts, makes an acceptable, calm base near the sea and the basilica pilgrimage site, as well as being within easy reach of Santa Cruz, the Esperanza woods and the National Park.
✉ 170 Avenida Generalísimo, Las Caletillas ☎ 922 50 02 00

La Laguna

Nivaria (££)
In a town with few hotels suitable for holidaymakers, the reasonably equipped three-star Aparthotel Nivaria is an acceptable possibility. It has no restaurant, but is well placed in the old centre of town close to all amenities.
✉ 11 Plaza del Adelantado ☎ 922 26 42 98

Santa Cruz de Tenerife

Atlántico (£)
This modest, pleasant, Spanish-oriented hotel, locally defined as a two-star, is adequately equipped, reasonably priced, and well placed in the main shopping street at the heart of the city.
✉ 12 Calle Castillo ☎ 922 24 63 75 Fax 922 24 63 78

Contemporanéo (£)
A modern three-star hotel almost free of English or German voices, located close to the Mencey, the García Sanabria park and the Rambla ring road. Rooms are pleasantly furnished and equipped, and there's a restaurant and snack bar.
✉ 116 Rambla General Franco ☎ 922 27 15 71 Fax 922 27 12 13

Escuela (££)
Unimaginative but reliable and comfortable, this four-star hotel in the west of the city is away from the heart of things, but offers good value for money.
✉ 152 Avenida San Sebastián ☎ 922 23 77 23

Mencey (£££)
Mencey means a Guanche chieftain, and this elegant, dignified and luxurious hotel is the chief among Tenerife's traditional five-star accommodation. In sumptuous colonial style with lavish marble, fine woodwork and artworks on display,the hotel offers every possible amenity: the location is peaceful, away from the city centre on the north side of the Ramblas.
✉ 38 Avenida Doctor José Naveiras ☎ 922 27 67 00 Fax 922 28 00 17

Pelinor (£)
This is a good example of a smaller, less expensive hotel, located in the heart of the city close to Plaza de España and aimed chiefly at Spanish visitors. The neat and comfort-able rooms have TV, and there's a bar on the premises.
✉ 8 Calle Béthencourt ☎ 922 24 68 75

Plaza (££)
Located in an agreeable square in the centre of the city, close to shops, restaurants and entertainment, this comfortable, reasonably priced hotel appeals more to business travellers than to holidaymakers, but makes a good base in the city.
✉ 10 Plaza de la Candelaria ☎ 922 27 24 53 Fax 922 27 51 60

The West

Garachico

San Roque (££)

One of the most unusual and delightful hotels on the island is this converted historic building in the middle of an interesting waterfront town. Though only three-star, the place has an exquisite low-key elegance, with plenty of polished wood, white fabric and minimalist décor. Armchairs and potted plants are dotted about, and there's a lovely arcaded and balconied open courtyard at the middle of the building. There are 20 rooms, with CD player, satellite TV and video.

32 Calle Esteban de Ponte
922 13 34 35 All year

Los Gigantes/Puerto de Santiago

Barceló Santiago (££)

A popular, large (yet low-rise) hotel belonging to the Barceló group and featured by several tour operators, this well-managed complex offers two pools, floodlit tennis courts, a restaurant, bars, evening entertainment and other facilities. The accommodation, in blocks around the pool area, consists of smallish but neat and adequate rooms.

8 La Hondura, Los Gigantes
922 10 09 12 Fax 922 10 18 08

Parque Nacional del Teide (El Teide National Park)

Parador las Cañadas del Teide (£–££)

While Spain's state-owned *paradors* are generally luxurious and expensive, this one is an inexpensive and unpretentious two-star hotel. Standing beside the National Park's through road, it's high in the volcanic interior of the island, very close to El Teide and the Park's other sights. It has 45 comfortable rooms, and is equipped with a pool and restaurant. It's popular with walkers rather than sun-seekers.

Parque Nacional del Teide
922 38 37 11 or 38 78 37

Puerto de la Cruz

Atlantis (££)

A reliable, comfortable, conventional holiday hotel by the sea, very well placed next to Playa Martiánez. Rooms are properly equipped, and there are two good pools, gardens, a gym, evening shows, and a buffet restaurant.

Calle Venezuela
922 37 45 45

Botánico (£££)

An exceptional hotel of relaxed elegance, offering the height of luxury and modern facilities combined with an easy-going enjoyment of the good things in life. On the northeast side of town, it's quite a long way from the centre and from the sea. Five stars, and a member of the Leading Hotels of the World group.

1 Avenida Richard Yeoward, Urbanización Botánico 922 38 14 00 Fax 922 38 15 04

Condesa (£)

Situated alongside the town's other two old hotels (the Marquesa and Monopol, ➤ 102) in the busy historic lower town, the rates here are inexpensive for a decent three-star hotel, and it retains plenty of old-style charm.

13 Calle Quintana
922 38 10 50 Fax 922 38 69 50

No Contest

The Spanish 'conquest' of the islands took several years as the Guanches put up fierce resistance in places. This is remarkable not least for the fact that the Guanches had almost no proper weapons. While the *conquistadores* wore armour and fought with guns, the Guanches responded by throwing stones or primitive wooden spears or defending themselves with clubs. Despite this, they proved hard to defeat and even won occasional victories over Spanish forces.

El Calabazo

Water is scarce on the Canaries. To deal with the problem, Tenerife farmers used a simple method of scooping water from canals, irrigation ditches or waterways into a tank and taking it to their crops. The men who scooped the water became very skilled, and were called *calabaceros*. The practice died out in the 1970s, but *calabazo* contests have become common at fiestas, with contestants seeing how quickly they can transfer water with a scoop. The scoops today are usually metal bowls, but the traditional tool was, of course, a *calabazo* (pumpkin).

Speak the Language?

The official language of the Canaries is Castilian Spanish, but the local dialect has many distinguishing features. Most striking is the complete absence of the normal Spanish 'th' sound (as in 'think'), which is usually written as 'ce'. In the Canaries, the letters 'ce' are pronounced as 's'. Another characteristic is the frequent use of Portuguese words, the result of the close relations between the Canaries and Latin America.

Strip off

Topless sunbathing is acceptable at all Tenerife beaches, pools and lidos, especially at the main resorts. Naturism, or stripping off completely, is never acceptable on resort beaches, but common on any secluded stretch of coast, or beaches outside resorts. Certain hotels at Puerto de la Cruz and Playa de las Américas have secluded separate sunbathing terraces specifically for nude sunbathing

Dania Park, Magec Park and Magec (££)

These three sister hotels face each other across the enticingly named Calle Cupido (Cupid Street). Set well back from the sea and a few minutes walk from the heart of town, these are decent mid-range tourist hotels, with a range of facilities, including restaurants, entertainment, rooftop pools and an area for nude sunbathing.
Guests at any of these establishments are free to use all the facilities of the others.

✉ 11 Calle Cupido
☎ 922 38 40 40

Marquesa (£–££)

The waterfront street of the original Puerto saw the creation of this hotel in 1712, long before the advent of tourism. It's been a hotel ever since, still relatively simple, but much modernised, with a swimming pool and restaurant. It's thoroughly charming, and keeps much of its colonial-era atmosphere.

✉ 11 Calle Quintana
☎ 922 38 31 51 Fax 922 38 69 50

Monopol (£–££)

One of the town's earliest hotels, down by the waterfront in the historic heart of town. Though much modernised, including the installation of a swimming pool, it retains a pleasing colonial feel, with cane furnishings and greenery in a charming patio.

✉ 15 Calle Quintana
☎ 922 38 46 11 Fax 922 37 03 10

Playa Canaria (££)

Despite the name, this hotel is a long way from the sea, in a quiet development at the back of town with views of El Teide and the green terraced fields of the Orotava Valley. A decent, modern, mid-range place, with a touch of Canarian style and a reasonable selection of facilities, it caters well for family holidaymakers.

✉ Urbanización El Duranzo
☎ 922 38 51 51 Fax 922 37 47 60

San Felipe (£££)

One of Puerto's best hotels, long established but thoroughly modernised, the high-rise San Felipe is owned by the prestigious Melia group. A huge range of facilities and services is on offer, with children's activities, and nightly entertainment, and rooms are well equipped. Close to the sea, the hotel is not far from the Playa Martiánez and the promenade, of which it has fine views. The Lido and town centre are only a short stroll away.

✉ 22 Avenida de Colón
☎ 922 38 33 11 Fax 922 37 37 18

Semiramis (£££)

Puerto's newest five-star, up the coast from Playa Martiánez, is some distance from the centre of town but has fine sea views from some rooms and offers every modern comfort and facility.

✉ Leopoldo Cólogan Zulueta
☎ 922 38 55 51 Fax 922 38 52 53

Tigaiga (££)

In the gorgeous garden setting of the Taoro Park area, above the town, this conventional tourist hotel has won awards for its environmental management. One of its claims is that the hotel has more palm trees than beds. Unremarkable but comfortable rooms have partial sea views and face either the Taoro Park or El Teide. The pool area has a view over Puerto, and there's a separate terrace for topless sunbathing.

✉ 28 Parque Taoro
☎ 922 38 35 00 Fax 922 38 40 55

The South

Costa Adeje

Anthelia Park (£££)

This grandiose modern resort complex consists of six small hotel blocks catering to slightly different markets. For example, one is for families, one is quiet, one consists only of luxury suites and so on. All the rooms have a sea view, and the whole place is equipped with a wealth of amenities and services. There are five pools, three restaurants, several bars, a kindergarten and a night club, as well as more unusual features, such as a library. Playa del Duque is a few minutes walk away.

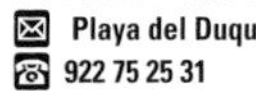

✉ Playa del Duque
☎ 922 75 25 31

Castalia Park (££)

Situated a block back from Playa de la Fañabé beach in Costa Adeje, this pleasant little aparthotel is a hit with families. The attractive low-rise balconied accommodation block curves attractively around its sunny pool area.

✉ 5 Calle Bruselas
☎ 922 71 33 66

Colón Guanahani (££)

An attractive low-rise building in neo-classical style, with marble and columns and arches, this hotel is in the western part of Costa Adeje. Green tile pathways wander among shrubs and palm trees, and the heated seawater pool is pleasant with surrounding trees. There's a good restaurant, plenty of facilities, entertainment and a children's club. Playa de la Fañabé is about 150m away.

✉ Playa de la Fañabé ☎ 922 71 28 14 Fax 922 71 21 21

Gran Hotel Bahía del Duque (£££)

The charming and attractive design of the building, which is along traditional Canarian lines, belies the fact that this is a large modern resort hotel of high standard. Located at the western edge of Costa Adeje, the hotel offers a wide array of facilities, including five pools, a fitness centre, beautiful gardens, six restaurants and much more.

✉ Playa del Duque–Fañabé
☎ 922 71 30 00 Fax 922 74 69 16

Jardín Tropical (£££)

Located at the Puerto Colón end of the Playa de Troya, where Playa de las Américas meets more up-market Costa Adeje, the award-winning Jardín Tropical is a superb resort hotel. Its imaginative white Moorish appearance, beautiful pool area, lush colourful vegetation and seafront location add up to a wonderful, luxurious place to stay on the south coast. There are five restaurants within the hotel.

✉ Calle Gran Bretaña
☎ 922 74 60 00

Jardines de Nivaria (£££)

Situated over in the quieter, western end of the resort, near Playa del Duque and Playa de la Fañabé, the designers of this hotel have tried to incorporate some local themes into its architectural design. Tiles and polished wood feature in the rooms. There is an attractive pool area, with seawater pools (one heated in winter), and many facilities.

✉ Calle Paris ☎ 922 71 33 33 Fax 922 71 33 40

Package Deal

Playa de las Américas, Costa Adeje and Los Cristianos run into each other along the coast, effectively creating a single resort area – often known collectively as Playa de las Américas. Only Los Cristianos had any existence before the tourism boom took off in the 1970s. Today the three areas consist almost entirely of scores of hotels, holiday apartments and 'aparthotels'. Almost all visitors arrive on an inclusive package with pre-booked accommodation – and that is the simplest and cheapest way to come to this part of Tenerife. However, the hotels listed here can all be booked independently, as well as being available through tour operators.

Golf Coast
Several golf links are located around Playa de las Américas. Just east of the resort, the quiet new villa and hotel development of Golf del Sur, though in a rather bleak location close to the former fishing village of Los Abrigos, has the advantage of being only 5km from Reina Sofía airport and near to high-quality golf links.

La Pinta (££)
Much of the accommodation in Playa de las Américas, Adeje and Los Cristianos is budget-priced aparthotels, combining self-catering and hotel. This is one of the better examples, with excellent facilities, pleasant dining room and pool area, and close to the seafront
✉ Urbanización San Eugenio ☎ 922 79 58 58

Golf del Sur

Las Adelfas (££)
Near the airport and Los Abrigos village, the aparthotel borders the PGA-approved 27-hole Golf del Sur course which has hosted the Tenerife Open. Accommodation is in a cluster of two-storey blocks designed to look like Spanish villas. They have fully fitted kitchens, tasteful simple furnishings and satellite TV, and enclose pools, a restaurant and a bar.
✉ Urbanización Golf del Sur (take San Miguel de Abona turn off highway) ☎ 922 73 86 16

Tenerife Golf (££)
The hotel stands at the seafront of this new coastal development near the airport, with air-conditioned rooms, all with balcony and cable TV. There's a buffet restaurant, a seawater pool (heated in winter), tennis court and entertainment.
✉ Urbanización Golf del Sur (take San Miguel de Abona turn off highway) ☎ 922 73 85 66 Fax 922 73 88 89

Los Cristianos

Tenerife Sur (££) and Cristian Sur (££)
These two aparthotels stand near each other at the back of the resort. Both have a lovely pool area, as well as games room, sauna, restaurant and supermarket Accommodation is in comfortable suites – not large, but all elegantly furnished and well equipped.
✉ Off Avenida de los Cristianos ☎ Tenerife Sur 922 79 14 74, Cristian Sur 922 79 26 00

Playa de las Américas

Bitácora (££)
One of the big popular holiday hotels, the Bitácora has a spacious pool and lawn, plenty of attractions and facilities for families and generous buffets.
✉ 1 Avenida Antonio Domíguez Alfonso ☎ 922 79 15 40 Fax 922 79 66 77

Las Dalias (££)
The huge and popular Las Dalias (800 beds) offers a poolside terrace, paella at the afternoon barbecue and a nightly disco. Nearby Los Hibiscos, Bougainville Playa and Torviscas Playa hotels are similar – all are in the Sungarden group, and all use the same booking numbers.
✉ Urbanización San Eugenio ☎ 922 79 27 12. Bookings 922 75 27 26, 922 75 26 04 Fax 922 75 08 76

Ponderosa (££)
Set well back from the sea, this modern, elegant hotel has 150 rooms, all attractive, tastefully decorated, well equipped and with good views. There's a restaurant and pleasant pool area and it's around a 300m walk to all the entertainment of the town centre.
✉ Calle Venezuela ☎ 922 79 02 04 Fax 922 79 54 72

Volcano (££)
This is a large, popular four-star hotel just a few minutes' walk from the beach, with lovely pools set amongst plenty of greenery, extensive facilities, entertainment and dancing.
✉ 8 Avenida Antonio Domínguez Alfonso ☎ 922 79 20 35 Fax 922 79 28 53

La Gomera

There are only a limited number of hotels and pensiones on the island of La Gomera, and most of the accomodation available involves staying in homes or private apartments. *Casas rurales* are former farmhouses now converted to rental properties; phone for reservations on ☎ **922 14 41 01**. A selection of good hotels are listed below.

Playa de Santiago

Hotel Jardín Tecina (£££)

This top class hotel in Playa de Santiago clings to a clifftop, with magnificent gardens of native plantlife (everything is labelled, as in a botanical park). It has a beautiful pool, and stirring views over the strait to Tenerife with El Teide rising in the distance. It's a truly impressive hotel, where the 'rooms' are in delightful cottages in the grounds.

✉ **Lomada de Tecina, Playa de Santiago** ☎ **922 14 58 50 Fax 922 14 58 51**

San Sebastián

Garajonay (££)

A modest and unpretentious old-style hotel with simple, clean and adequate bedrooms – but no frills: no restaurant, no bar, and some rooms without a bathroom. What it does have are peace and quiet, a friendly, untouristy atmosphere, a central position and very moderate prices.

✉ **17 Ruiz de Parón, San Sebastián** ☎ **922 87 05 50 Fax 922 87 05 50**

Parador de San Sebastián de la Gomera (£££)

The best and most luxurious *parador* in the Canaries, and indeed one of the most appealing in all Spain, is to be found here on La Gomera. Built on a hill grandly overlooking the town and port, it has an air of elegance and history, and is meticulously furnished and decorated in the style of the Canaries' finest early colonial mansions of the 1570s, resembling the home of a Spanish nobleman. Astonishingly, the whole thing was created in the late 1970s! The use of dark woods for panelling, bare polished boards, sumptuous fabrics, displays of historical pictures and artefacts, including portraits of Christopher Columbus (➤ 14) and 15th-century local countess Beatriz de Bombadilla, all deliberately create the impression of antiquity. The central courtyard is pretty with greenery, and outside there are formal gardens. The house is small (another authentic touch), so you'll have to book well ahead to be sure of a room here. More modern features include every comfort in the bedrooms, and a swimming pool.

✉ **Balcón de la Villa y Puerto, Lomo de la Horca** ☎ **922 87 11 00 Fax 922 87 11 16**

Villa Gomera (£)

Standing on a San Sebastián street where many traditional low-key family-run hotels can be found (➤ Garajonay above), this is a small, friendly establisment and makes a pleasant base.

✉ **68 Ruiz de Parón, San Sebastián** ☎ **922 87 00 20 Fax 922 87 02 35**

Class Act

Playa de las Américas, the ultimate mass-market resort, has good family accommodation and entertainment but also has its share of bierkellers, lager louts and garish late-night entertainment. Los Cristianos, east of Playa, has always been considered a little more select. In contrast to these two, the newer development of Costa Adeje, on the other side of Playa, aims to be a little classier, with higher prices, more style, some beautiful landscaping and several grandiose, neo-classical modern hotels. Beware, though, of falling under the spell of free gifts and holiday dreams.

Children's Attractions

Home from Home
Families with young children should consider self-catering in preference to hotel accommodation. Tenerife has plenty of holiday apartments and aparthotels, combining small self-catering suites with some hotel facilities. The home-from-home freedom makes life much easier than sticking to hotel routines. To pre-book self-catering accommodation, one specialist company is Casas Canarias in London ☎ 0171 485 4387.

The island provides little that is especially for children, but it doesn't need to – most of Tenerife's attractions are a are a big hit with people of all ages.

Amazing Plants

Plant life in Tenerife is not just of interest to gardeners – some of it's weird enough even to grab the attention of children.

Bananera El Guanche
(► 55) All about bananas...and other plants.
✉ 2km from Puerto de la Cruz, on road to La Orotava ☎ 922 33 18 53 🕑 Daily 9–6

Drago Milenario(► 17, Top Ten) One of the largest and oldest specimens of this curious species.
✉ Icod de las Vinos 🚌 354 and 363 from Puerto de la Cruz

Jardin Botánico (► 58)
Children and adults will enjoy this exotic city park.
✉ Calle Retama, off Carretara del Botánico, Puerto de la Cruz 🕑 Daily 9–6

Jardines del Atlántico
Another chance to go bananas at these lush gardens on the South coast.
✉ Exit 26 of Autopista del Sur ☎ 922 72 04 03 🕑 Tours at 10, 11:30, 1, 2:15 and 3:30

Parque Nacional de Garajonay, La Gomera
(► 26, Top Ten) The twisting branches of the forest are like scenes from a movie.
✉ Juego de Bolas, La Gomera

Animal Parks

Amazonia Parques Exóticos
Cactus and animal park, including a reptilarium.
✉ Near Exit 26 on Autopista (motorway) ☎ 922 79 54 24 🕑 Daily 10–7 🚌 Free shuttle bus from Playa de las Américas and Los Cristianos

Loro Parque
Tropical wonderland of animals and birds, including performing dolphins, parrots, gorillas, tigers, monkeys, penguins and flamingos (► 21, Top Ten).
✉ 3km west of Puerto de la Cruz, near Punta Brava ☎ 922 37 38 41, 922 37 40 81 🕑 Daily 8:30–5 🚌 Free shuttle from Avenida de Venezuela (near Lido) and Plaza del Charco, Puerto de la Cruz

Parque Ecológico Aguilas del Teide
See condors and crocodiles, elephants, eagles and penguins in this dramatic tropical park, where in five display areas creatures put on performances every evening. Feeding times are particularly worth seeing. Also on the site: dodgem boats and other amusements (► 75).
✉ On Arona road just out of Los Cristianos ☎ 922 75 30 01 🕑 Daily 10–6 🚌 Free shuttle bus from Playa de las Américas and Los Cristianos

Zoolandia
Appealing zoo with pony rides.
✉ On Autopista (motorway) just north of Puerto de la Cruz ☎ 922 33 35 09 🕑 Daily 9–6 🚌 Free shuttle bus from Playa Martiánez in Puerto de la Cruz

Camel Rides

Camel Park
A farm in the sun, breeding camels, making wine, growing local crops and

selling island crafts. One of their principal activities is mini-excursions by camel.
✉ La Camela, off Autopista (motorway) near Los Cristianos ☎ 922 72 10 80 ⊕ Daily 10–5 🚌 Free shuttle buses from Los Cristianos and Playa de las Américas

Camello Center
Hold on tight for camel rides and donkey safaris at La Tanque, near Garachico. Afterwards have tea in an Arab tent .
✉ La Tanque (east of Garachico) ☎ 922 83 11 91 ⊕ Daily 10–6

Eating Out
Restaurants think nothing of catering for children in the evening. Even at home, children are often up playing while the grown-ups talk until late. It's taken for granted that children are a constant part of family life. Children are welcome in bars and restaurants, and indulged with courtesy and kindness. However, restaurants, bars and cafés *don't* generally list children's menus, or provide dishes specially for children; instead, children are given small portions of whatever they fancy.

Fiesta Magic
Come to Tenerife during the Santa Cruz Carnaval (early to miid-Feb) for a wild week of mayhem and all-night revelry that will thrill older children (though might not appeal to younger ones). Failing that, find a fiesta during your visit – the noise, amusements, music and crowds provide unforgettable memories.

Meeting Whales and Dolphins
Children will love going out on the sea trips to experience an encounter with whales or dolphins (► 111). About 200 pilot whales are living in Canary Island waters and tend to stay on the south side of the archipelago. An easy place to spot whales is between Los Cristianos and Los Gigantes, where dolphins can also be found. Boat trips to see them are among the highlights for visitors. The same trips often offer glass-bottomed or glass-sided viewing so that, even if whales and dolphins are not sighted, there is much to see and enjoy.

Under the Sea
Yellow Submarine
A submarine adventure takes you exploring among the depths of the sea.
✉ South Pier, Puerto Colón, Playa de las Américas ☎ 922 71 50 80 (Reservation advised) ⊕ Daily 10–6 🚌 Free shuttle bus from Puerto Colón to Playa de las Américas, Los Cristianos, Costa Adeje and Aguapark Octopus

Water Fun
Aguapark Octopus
This water amusement park offers slides, pools, dolphin shows and water features. Plan to spend at least half a day; you can have a meal here too (► 74).
✉ San Eugenio Alto, Costa Adeje/Playa de las Américas (near Exit 29 of the Autopista) ☎ 922 71 52 66, or 922 71 42 70; fax 922 71 48 03 ⊕ Daily 10–6 🚌 Free shuttle bus to Playa de las Américas and several other resorts

On Film
El Teide National Park (► oo) is a good choice for a day out with aspiring young movie buffs. Intended to convey a primeval wilderness, it has featured as a background in *The Ten Commandments* and *Planet of the Apes*. In the film *One Million Years BC*, Raquel Welch could be seen here wearing only a fur bikini.

Handicrafts & Souvenirs

A Taste of Honey

One of the strangest specialities in the Canaries is the palm-tree 'honey' of La Gomera. Not real honey, Miel de Palma is made like maple syrup. The *guarapo*, or sap, of the date palm is tapped, then boiled. The result is a dark paste that is rich, tasty and sweet. Buy it where you see signs at smallholdings around the island, or in San Sebastián at the market.

Duty and Tax

Although the Canaries are a duty-free area, it doesn't follow that all goods are free of tax. Prices are bumped up by the local IGIC tax, which puts 4 per cent on the value of goods and is sometimes not included in window-display price tags.

Embroidery, Lace and Threadwork

The Canaries are known for exquisite embroidery (*bordados*) and fine threadwork (*calados*) and decorative lacework, especially doilies (*rosetas*). Exceptional patience, skill, delicacy and care are required of the local women who do the work. However, you should beware of street sellers and market traders offering very inferior low-priced imported factory-made embroidery and claiming that it is genuine local craftwork.

Pottery

Canarian potters traditionally didn't use the potter's wheel, and still today on Tenerife and La Gomera highly skilled local potters working entirely by hand produce distinctive household objects and decorative items. Look out in the craft shops for their *gánigos* – household pots made without a potter's wheel – and necklaces and other jewellery decorated with Guanche symbols.

Wickerwork

Local handmade Tenerife basketwork is distinctive and pretty, and makes a good choice for souvenirs. Skilled wickerwork craftsmen and women can be seen working in the many craft fairs.

Shops

A range of all these locally made items can be found at the following craft stores. It may be worth shopping around, as the stock varies from place to place. Shop hours are generally Mon–Sat 9:30–1, 3–6:30.

The North

A fine selection of Canarian crafts is available at the following stores:

Arte Tenerife
☒ Plaza de España, Santa Cruz

Artesanía Celsa
☒ 8 Calle Castillo, Santa Cruz

La Casa de los Balcones
☒ Edificio Olimpo, Plaza de la Candelaria, Santa Cruz

La Casa de los Calados
☒ 9 Calle Núñez de la Peña, La Laguna

Mercado de Artesanía Española
☒ 8 Plaza de la Candelaria, Santa Cruz

The West

Casa de los Balcones

This beautifully restored 17th-century mansion (► 16, Top Ten) contains a craft shop, where local people can often be seen at work. As well as cheap souvenirs, a wide range of high-quality items, such as Spanish and Canarian lace and linen and traditional Canarian embroideries, are on sale. Some are made on the premises, as the Casa de los Balcones also serves as a highly regarded school of embroidery.
☒ 3 Calle San Francisco, La Orotava

Casa Iriarte
The disorganised store in this historic building has a fine selection of hand-worked table linen.
✉ **17 Calle San Juan, Puerto de la Cruz**

La Casa del Turista
Located opposite La Orotava's famous Casa de los Balcones (► 108), this craft and souvenir shop has the same owners and stocks similar products.
✉ **Calle San Francisco, La Orotava**

Casa Torrehermosa
The most important craft shop on the island, a jealous guardian of authenticity and tradition. It is run by the state-run crafts organisation, the Empresa Insular de Artesanía del Cabildo de Tenerife, and specialises in genuine local work. There is a craft museum attached.
✉ **27 Calle Tomás Zerolo, La Orotava** ☎ **922 33 40 13**

The following shops also have a good range of craft products:

Artesanía del Lino
✉ **Calle Santo Domingo, Puerto de la Cruz**

La Casa de los Balcones
✉ **Paseo de San Telmo, Puerto de la Cruz**

The South

La Casa de los Balcones
This shop knows its market, with a wide range of inexpensive craftworks that double as souvenirs.
✉ **Shopping Centre, Playa de las Américas**

Mercado de Artesanía Española
An interesting placeon the way into the El Teide National Park.
✉ **Carretera General de Arona, Vilaflor** 🕐 **All year**

La Gomera

Artesanía Los Telares
See weaving and other local crafts in production before you buy. There is a similar *artenesía* at Agulo, the next village about 3km away.
✉ **Hermigua** 🕐 **Mon–Sat**

Market
Gomeran craftwork and local products at morning market.
✉ **Avenida de Colón, San Sebastián**

Summer Fairs

Have fun while looking for souvenirs at these isummer fairs, or *ferias artesanía.*

Los Realejos	**May, Jun**
Güimar	**Jun**
La Orotava	**Jun**
El Sauzal	**Jun/July**
La Laguna	**Jul**
Santiago del Teide	**Jul**
Arona/Los Cristianos	**Jul/Aug**
Fasnia	**Aug**
El Rosario	**Aug**
Garachico	**Aug**
La Victoria de Acentejo	**Aug**
Buenavista del Norte	**Aug**
La Matanza	**Aug**
Vilaflor	**Aug/Sep**
San Juan de la Rambla	**Sep**
San Miguel de Abona	**Sep**
Guía de Isora	**Sep**
Tacoronte	**Sep**
El Tanque	**Oct**

Unusual Souvenirs

Choose from banana-shaped bottles of sugary *cobana* (banana liqueur), dolls in national costume, items made from palm leaves, or banana-leaf baskets. On a more serious level, there is a wide range of high-quality local pottery items, linen goods or lacy handmade handkerchiefs, napkins, placemats and tablecloths. Lace and embroidered goods can be found in craft shops (► above); other items are sold not just in dedicated souvenir shops but also in garages, newsagents, and supermarkets.

Gomeran Pots
La Gomera retains many ancient qualities, including the making of handmade pots without a potter's wheel. One of the villages best known for this is tiny El Cercado, high on a narrow, winding road in the west of the island. Many of its simple cottages are pottery workshops, where the pots are made from the island's striking dark red clay.

Hypermarket Shopping
Self-caterers and others will sometimes prefer to go to a supermarket to make shopping easy. The Continente *centro commercial* not only has a huge hypermarket with a vast range of goods at reasonable prices, but there are also 150 other shops on the site. The Continente 6km south of Santa Cruz by the Santa Maria del Mar exit from the Autopista del Sur (South Motorway).
🕐 Mon–Sat 10–10

Bargains and Markets

Out of Africa
Colourfully dressed West Africans hawking on the beaches, in the streets and selling in the markets and fairs of Tenerife bring an exotic note. These traders are often Senegalese, make the boat trip specifically to sell in European markets and stay for several months. Usually they all sell very similar goods: leatherwork, carved toys, African drums, beads and, at higher prices, often illegally exported tribal artefacts, including ceremonial masks. What not to buy: ivory – many African traders offer ivory items, but these are illegal throughout the EU, with heavy fines and confiscation of the goods if found by customs officers.

Bargains

As a duty-free region, the Canary Islands are like a big duty-free shop, selling perfumes, cameras, binoculars and other optical goods, CD-players and electronic items, at lower prices than at home. In the big towns and main resorts, several Asian–run 'Bazaars' are the usual outlet for these goods. With their big Tax Free Shopping signs and offers of amazing bargains, these shops are virtually identical and have the same range of stock. Marked prices are generally open to a bit of haggling, though some stores make a point of not negotiating – a selling point with Europeans who dread haggling! Prices are similar to those in airport shops and other duty-free outlets. Before buying, it helps to know what the price is back home, and whether the guarantee will be valid. The main outlets are: Callede Castillo, Santa Cruz; Playa de las Américas; Puerto de la Cruz.

Markets and Hawkers

Genuine markets like Mercado Nuestra Señora de África in Santa Cruz (► 23, Top Ten) are the place to find fresh fruit and vegetables and kitchenware, fabrics and household items. Most other Tenerife markets attract European hippy 'artists' and African traders, selling a repetitive range of kitsch, beads and home-made jewellery, and leather goods. Some of them occasionally offer original or interesting items. They are often joined by Spanish stallholders offering either bargain clothes, beachwear, etc,, or lace, crochet and embroidery, especially tablecloths, placemats, napkins, bedlinen and handkerchiefs. These are not always offered at low prices, but they represent good value for such high-quality handmade work.You may also find glazed pottery and crockery, attractively hand-painted. When not at the markets, the hippies and African traders often hawk their goods in streets and on the beaches.

Main Markets

Los Abrigos
Night market, Tue 6–10

Playa de las Américas and Los Cristianos
Next to Hotel Gran Arona, Los Cristianos, Sun 9–2
Torviscas, Playa de las Américas Thu and Sat 9–2

Puerto de la Cruz
In market building, Avenida de Blas Pérez Gonzáles, Mon–Sat AM (☎ 922 38 61 58)

Santa Cruz
Mercado Nuestra Señora de África, Calle de San Sebastián. Mon–Sat 8–1
Rastro, or flea market, outside the Mercado. Sun 10–2

San Sebastián, La Gomera
Avenida de Colón, Mon–Sat mornings

Tacoronte
Rustic farmers' market, Sat PM, Sun AM

Excursions

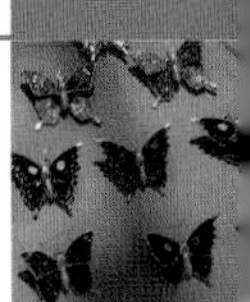

Arts and Drama

Tenerife has several art galleries, museums, concert halls and theatres. Most of the island's culture is firmly located in the north, well away from the tourist sites.

La Laguna

The town of La Laguna, little frequented by tourists, is Tenerife's centre of high culture. Each year it hosts the island's Jazz Festival and International Theatre Festival
Teatro Leal ✉ **Calle Obispo Rey Redondo, La Laguna**

Santa Cruz

Teatro Guimerá
Plays (Spanish-language only), opera and concerts – and home of the first-class Symphony Orchestra of Tenerife, which gives performances all year.
✉ **Plaza Isla de la Madera, Santa Cruz** ☎ **922 60 62 65**

Boat Excursions

Several tour operators and local travel firms organise boat excursions from Los Cristianos, Playa de las Américas, Costa Adeje and Costa del Silencio. Day trips to La Gomera are especially popular and enjoyable. Other boat trips have no goal except fun, such as the many Sangria Excursions, Pirate Adventures, etc, which include lunch and usually a swimming stop.

Yellow Submarine
A trip in a semi-submersible to find out what lives in the seas around southern Tenerife (► 107).
✉ **South Pier, Puerto Colón, Playa de las Américas** ☎ **922 71 50 80 (Reservation advised)**
🕘 **Daily 10–6**

Tours

Organised bus or coach tours are a popular way of exploring the varied scenery and landscapes of Tenerife. For suggested destinations, ► panel.

Whalewatching

About 200 pilot whales are living in Canary Island waters and tend to stay on the south side of the archipelago. An easy place to spot whales is between Los Cristianos and Los Gigantes; dolphins can also be found. Boat trips to see them are among the island's highlights for visitors. The same trips often offer glass-bottomed or glass-sided viewing so that, even if whales and dolphins are not sighted, there is much to see and enjoy.

Nostramo
Successful and popular boat excursions in a beautiful sailing ship, a Spanish schooner built in 1918. As well as seeing dolphins and whales, the outing is civilised, elegant and unforgettable. During a leisurely trip below the Los Gigantes cliffs, lunch is served on board, and there's a pause in Masca Bay for a chance to swim.
✉ **Playa San Juan, Playa de las Américas** ☎ **922 75 00 85 in Playa de las Américas, 922 38 51 16 in Puerto de la Cruz**
🕘 **Departs daily 10AM**

Tropical Delfin
Modern excursion boat with experienced crew. The 36 big underwater windows give a chance to see the sea; keep a look out for dolphins.
✉ **South Pier, Puerto Colón, Playa de las Américas** ☎ **922 75 01 49** 🕘 **Daily 11–1**

Coach Tours
The most rewarding tours include a trip to El Teide; across the Macizo de Teno to Buenavista; and a day out in Santa Cruz. If you are staying in Playa de las Américas, a day trip to Puerto, including Loro Parque and Bananera, is highly enjoyable. Another worthwhile tour is the day out on La Gomera. These tours are available from hotel reception desks and through tour operators' reps at the resorts.

Whalewatching Tips
- Only travel with boat firms licensed to run excursions (like the two included on this page).
- Boats should not get too close to whales.
- Engines should be turned off when near whales.
- Don't change direction frequently – this irritates the whales.
- Don't throw anything at whales (and do not throw litter into the sea).
- Don't swim with whales – remember, they are wild animals.

Sport

Peaceful Island
In contrast to the lively scene on its larger neighbour, little La Gomera has almost no organised sport, entertainment or nightlife. Some of the hotels do put on low-key shows, and there are small discos. Tourists, like locals, must rely on fiestas for music, folklore and fun.

Golf

Many visitors come to Tenerife purely in order to play golf on the island's six excellent golf courses, four of which are in the area between Playa de las Américas and the airport. If you are playing and staying in the south, visit the northern golf course at least once – for the amazing contrast of lush greenery. Each of the golf courses has formed partnerships with many nearby hotels, whose resident guests enjoy reduced green fees (enquire at the clubs for current details).

North

Real Club de Golf Tenerife
An 18-hole course founded in 1932 by British expatriates. There is a green fee of 6,500 ptas per day.
✉ El Peñon, Tacoronte (2km from Los Rodeos airport, 14km from Santa Cruz) ☎ 922 25 02 40

South

Amarilla Golf
An 18-hole seashore course, bordered by cliffs and luxury housing. A green fee of 5,900–8,400 ptas applies, according to the season.
✉ Urbanización Amarilla Golf, San Miguel de Abona ☎ 922 79 24 61 / 922 79 35 59 / 922 78 57 77

Golf del Sur
This course has hosted several international events. There are 27 holes and a green fee of 6,100–8,150 ptas per day according to the season.
✉ Urbanización Golf del Sur, San Miguel de Abona ☎ 922 70 45 55

Costa Adeje Golf
An eighteen-hole new site, planning to increase to 27 holes. Greens are large, with several doglegs. Located only 5km from Playa de las Américas, with views of La Gomera.
✉ Finca de los Olivos, Adeje ☎ 922 71 08 79

Golf Las Américas
A 72-par course just outside Playa de las Américas and Los Cristianos; 18 holes. Green fee 10,000 ptas per day.
✉ Take Exit 28 from the Autopista (motorway) and follow sign ☎ 922 75 20 05

Los Palos Centro de Golf
A par-27 nine-hole course five minutes from Playa de las Américas. Though small, the course offers plenty of challenges. Green fee 3,000 ptas for two rounds.
✉ At Arona, on Carretera Guaza–Las Galletas ☎ 922 73 00 80

Diving

Scuba and offshore diving is popular all around the islands, with several centres offering a good standard and staffed by qualified instructors.

Aden Tenerife Multi-Aventura
✉ 41 Calle Castillo (Oficina 307), Santa Cruz ☎ 922 24 62 61

Atlantik
✉ Hotel Maritim, 1 Calle El Burgado, Puerto de la Cruz ☎ 922 34 45 01

Centro Insular de Deportes
✉ Carretera Santa Cruz–San Andrés ☎ Fax 922 24 09 45

Club Nautico
✉ **Avenida de Anaga, Santa Cruz** ☎ **922 27 37 00.**

Club Nautico de Güimar
✉ **Apartado 19, Güimar**
☎ **922 52 89 00**

Go-Karting

Karting Club Tenerife
This club has one of the best kart circuits in Europe.
✉ **Carretera de Cho, at km 66, off the southern Autopista at Guaza** ☎ **922 78 66 20**

Riding

Several country stables and riding clubs organise enjoyable horseback excursions.

Aden Tenerife MultiAventura
✉ **41 Calle Castillo (Oficina 307), Santa Cruz** ☎ **922 24 62 61**

Club Hipico la Atalaya
✉ **1 Camino de San Lázaro, edge of Santa Cruz** ☎ **922 25 57 39**

El Rodeos de la Paja
✉ **Camino de la Villa, El Ortigal (near La Laguna)**
☎ **922 25 40 11**

Walking, Climbing, Cycling

Graded footpaths marked and maintained by ICONA, the Spanish conservation agency, criss-cross the island. They issue a number of maps (available in tourist offices on the island) showing marked walks.
For further advice on walking ➤ panel, (right).

Aden Tenerife MultiAventura
This highly proficient multi-adventure sports centre organises cycling tours, mountain cycling, walking excursions and climbing.
✉ **41 Calle Castillo (Oficina 307), Santa Cruz** ☎ **922 24 62 61**

Windsurfing, Surfing

Near-constant trade winds and warm unpolluted waters ensure ideal conditions for windsurfing and surfing around the island's south coast. One of the best locations is El Médano beach, on the south coast close to the airport. Waters on the north coast are too rough for safe surfing.

Centro Insular de Deportes
✉ **Carretera Santa Cruz–San Andrés** ☎ **922 24 09 45**

Sunwind
✉ **Avenida Islas Canarias, El Médano** ☎ **922 17 61 74**

Wrestling

One of the traditional island sports, called *La Lucha* or *Lucha Canaria*, is a curious form of wrestling. With its own weekly TV show, and frequent matches, Canarian Wrestling has become very popular in recent years.
Two teams compete by pitting one man against another, in turns, until there is a clear victory. The men, wearing a particular style of shorts and shirt, try to throw each other to the ground by gripping the side of each other's clothing. It is slow and careful, with sudden moves as the men try to catch each other off guard.
Tourists are welcome to watch matches: ask at hotels or tourist office for match details and venues.

Walking Advice
ICONA, the outdoor activities and conservation agency, give the following advice to walkers in Tenerife:
• Take a hat and sunglasses
• Take water to drink
• Don't pick any plants
• Let someone know about your walk
• Never walk without a map (available from Puerto de la Cruz and Santa Cruz tourist offices, and El Teide National Park Visitor Centre ☎ 922 29 01 29

Nightlife

A Night In
Most tourist hotels, especially the larger places, offer music, shows and entertainment on the premises every evening. Some can be quite spectacular, with a cabaret-style floorshow and dancers. Flamenco and colourful folklore shows are common. Several hotels also host loud, atmospheric discos for the younger crowd.

Champion Cocktail
Puerto's Casino Taoro won the 1988 Spanish National Cocktail Contest for its house drink, called Cocktail Taoro. It's a sizzling, hilarious, extravagant and drinkable mix of champagne, calvados and banana liqueur with lemon and caviar.

Casinos

Casino Playa de las Américas
Place your bets in the south of the island at Hotel Gran Tenerife.
✉ Avenida Maritima, Playa de las Américas ☎ 922 79 37 58

Casino Santa Cruz
Dress up for an evening of roulette, blackjack and poker at Tenerife's poshest hotel.
✉ Hotel Mencey, 38 Avenida Doctor José Naveiras, Santa Cruz ☎ 922 27 67 00

Casino Taoro
Tenerife's grandest casino, in Puerto de la Cruz, is housed in a former fine hotel that played host to Europe's nobility over a century ago. Although badly damaged by fire in 1929, the hotel's lavish architecture and wonderful location high in the Parque Taoro guaranteed its survival, and it reopened as a casino. Cocktails are served, there is a smart restaurant, and slot machines as well as roulette and gambling tables. Casual dressers are not admitted, there's a modest entrance charge, and you must take your passport.
✉ Carretera del Taoro, Puerto de la Cruz ☎ 922 38 05 50

Pubs, Clubs and Discos

Los Cristianos/Playa de las Américas
The Veronicas Strip on the Avenida Litoral in Playa de las Américas is the focal point for entertainment. Things liven up around 11PM. Many bars close at 3AM, but others stay open till 5 or 6AM.

Banana Garden
A (slightly) older group prefers this live and disco music venue.
✉ Veronicas, Playa de las Américas ☎ 922 79 03 65

La Divina Comedia
The grim face of Dante welcomes you to this disco.
✉ 11–12B Centro Commercial San Telmo, Los Cristianos

Linekers Bar
Booze, telly, bar food and good cheer at this noisily popular laddish football pub opposite Veronicas.
✉ Starco Commercial Centre, Playa de las Américas

Metropolis
There's a young party atmosphere at this popular pub disco. Sit and listen or get up and dance. Two rooms – one for house, and the other for live music and disco.
✉ Hotel Conquistador, Paseo Maritimo, Playa de las Américas ☎ 922 79 73 59

Prisma
✉ Hotel Tenerife Sol, Avenida Litoral, Playa de las Américas ☎ 922 79 10 70

Trauma
✉ Avenida Litoral, Playa de las Américas

Puerto de la Cruz
A quieter, slightly older holiday crowd frequents Puerto's late night venues.

Blue Not
Has the 'e' fallen off? No – that's the name of this well-known jazz spot.
✉ Calle Zamora

Catar
✉ Urbanización La Paz

Concordia
✉ **Avenida Venezuela**

Coto
✉ **Off Calle Aceviño, Urbanización La Paz**

Joy
✉ **Obispo Pérez Cáceres**

Royal Regins
✉ **Avenida Colón**

Victoria
✉ **Avenida Colón**

Santa Cruz
The clientele who jam into Santa Cruz's nightspots are mainly young Spanish visitors, plus the more adventurous among the foreign tourists, .

Daida
✉ **Residencia Anaga, Avenida Anaga**

Ku
✉ **Parque la Granja**

Noh
✉ **Avenida Anaga**

Nooctua
✉ **Avenida Anaga**

Dinner-Dance, Nightclubs and Cabaret
Known here as 'show restaurants', many places offer different styles of floorshows and entertainment while the audience is eating or drinking. Some are very slick, featuring international comedians, jugglers and other entertainers.
Others offer a more risqué type of performance, with the prettiest of showgirls dressed in feathers and not much else.

Santa Cruz and the North
Barbacoa
The name is Spanish for 'barbecue', summing up the style of food and the relaxed atmosphere of this show restaurant.
✉ **Tacoronte** ☎ **922 56 01 56**

Puerto de la Cruz and the West
Andromeda
This popular, stylish cabaret and show restaurant was created by artist César Manrique and is located at his Lido de Martiánez on the Puerto seafront. It attracts world-class artistes and highly professional dancers and showgirls. Dinner is at 8, and the floor show starts at 10.
✉ **Lido, Puerto de la Cruz**
☎ **922 38 38 52**

Tenerife Palace
✉ **Puerto de la Cruz** ☎ **922 38 29 60**

Playa de las Américas and the South
La Ballena
A show restaurant in Ten-Bel, on the Costa del Silencio.
✉ **Ten-Bel** ☎ **922 73 00 60**

Banana Garden
A show restaurant also offering a disco.
✉ **Playa de las Américas** ☎ **922 79 03 65**

Tablao Flamenco
See flamenco shows while you dine.
✉ **Parque las Américas, Playa de las Américas**

Theme Dinners
Castillo
You can pretend it's the Middle Ages in this mock-medieval castle and dine in jolly mood to the accompaniment of tournaments and boisterous family fun with music, singing and dancing.
✉ **San Miguel Aldea Blanca, San Miguel** ☎ **922 70 02 76**

A Night on the Town
In Puerto de la Cruz, nightlife is mainly focused on Avenida de Colón and its side turnings. It's relaxed, good-humoured and civilised, with live music bars and discos.
In Playa de las Américas, things are livelier, more raucous and harder-edged, with the centre of action being around the Veronicas complex. Here you'll find discos for all tastes, and fun pubs and bars where things get going after 11pm. To get away from tourists, visit Santa Cruz for cheaper discos and late-night bars – look along Avenida Anaga and Rambla del General Franco. Don't miss the city's open-air discos during high summer. However, Santa Cruz tends to be quiet at night during the week, livelier at weekends.

What's On When

Spit out the Old Year, Swallow the New
Locals have their own tradition which it's fun to share if you are here on New Year's Eve. As the clock strikes twelve and the new year begins, at every chime you should eat a grape and spit the seeds out. If you can do that without difficulty, you should also take a sip of cava at every one of the twelve chimes.

Carnival Month
The high point of the year for most Tenerife residents is the wild, colourful and sometimes frenzied week-long carnival in February. It's the second biggest carnival in the world after Rio, and draws immense crowds from all Spanish-speaking countries. The high point is Shrove Tuesday. Huge processions and parades, with participants dressed in fantastic costumes that have often taken the whole year to prepare, take over the capital city and to a lesser extent Tenerife's other big towns. The whole month is affected, as people take time off work to prepare, to celebrate – or to recover from staying up all night and enjoying drinks like the Carnival favourite, Cubata – rum and Coke.

These are the main events in a year packed with fiestas and festivities.

January
5–6 Jan: Cabalgata de los Reyes Magos (The Three Kings Cavalcade), in many places, especially Santa Cruz and Valle Gran Rey (La Gomera)
17–22 Jan: Local fiestas in Garachico, Icod de los Vinos, Los Realejos and San Sebastián (La Gomera)

February
The whole month is called Carnival Month, with a festive mood everywhere.
2 Feb: Candelaria, or Candlemas, big festival and pilgrimage in certain towns and villages, especially Candelaria
Early–mid Feb (around 8–15 Feb): one week Carnaval, Santa Cruz, and Puerto de la Cruz – huge events, parades, festivities. The climax is Shrove Tuesday, the biggest event of the year.
End Feb: Carnaval, Los Cristianos – marks the end of Tenerife's Carnival Month
End Feb/early Mar: Carnaval, San Sebastián (La Gomera)

March/April
19 Mar: San José holiday
Semana Santa (Holy Week): big events, often sober in character, all over the islands during Easter Week
25 Apr: Local fiestas especially at Icod de los Vinos, Teguesta and Agulo (La Gomera)

May/June
Late May/early Jun (c. 2 Jun): *Corpus Cristi*: Octavo (eight days) of huge celebrations throughout the island, especially La Orotava, La Laguna and Vilaflor. Streets are decorated with sand-and-flower designs
After Corpus Cristi: Romería – the season of local pilgrimages
24 Jun: Fiesta de San Juan, celebrating the midsummer at Vallehermoso (La Gomera) and other villages

July
15 Jul: Fiestas del Gran Poder: Puerto de la Cruz – processions, parades, fireworks and fun
25 Jul: Santiago: festive public holiday; in Santa Cruz, celebration of the defeat of Admiral Nelson

August
15 Aug: Asunción and Nuestra Señora de la Candelaria: Candelaria – important pilgrimage festival involving whole island
16 Aug: Romeria de San Roque: Garachico – popular, colourful local event
30 Aug: Nuestra Señora del Carmen: Los Cristianos – lively fiesta

September
1–6 Sep: Semana Colombina (Columbus Week), San Sebastián (La Gomera)
15 Sep: Virgen de Buen Paso: Alajeró (La Gomera)
Mid-Sep: Local fiestas at La Laguna and Tacoronte

October
1–6 Oct: Vergen de Guadaloupe: major festival all over La Gomera
12 Oct: Día de la Hispanidad: celebrating Columbus

November/December
Holidays on 1 Nov, 6 Dec, 8 Dec, 25 Dec, 28 Dec

Practical Matters

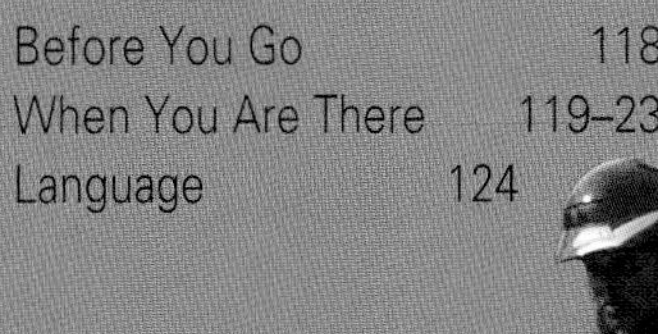

Above: *Windsurfers congregate at El Médano*
Right: *A scooter-borne timeshare salesperson*

TIME DIFFERENCES

GMT	Tenerife	California	USA (NY)	New Zealand	Spain
12 noon	12 noon	4AM	7AM	12 midnight	1PM

BEFORE YOU GO

WHAT YOU NEED

● Required
○ Suggested
▲ Not required

	UK	Germany	USA	Netherlands	Spain
Passport	●	●	●	●	●
Visa	▲	▲	▲	▲	▲
Onward or Return Ticket	●	●	○	●	●
Health Inoculations	▲	▲	▲	▲	▲
Health Documentation (➤ 123, Health)	▲	▲	▲	▲	▲
Travel Insurance	○	○	○	○	○
Driving Licence (national)	●	●	●	●	●
Car Insurance Certificate (if own car)	○	○	○	○	○
Car Registration Document (if own car)	●	●	●	●	●

WHEN TO GO

Tenerife

High season

Low season

JAN	FEB	MAR	APR	MAY	JUN	JUL	AUG	SEP	OCT	NOV	DEC
21°C	21°C	23°C	24°C	25°C	26°C	29°C	29°C	29°C	27°C	24°C	21°C

 Very wet  Wet  Cloud  Sun  Cloud/Sun

TOURIST OFFICES

In the UK
Spanish National Tourist Office
23 Manchester Square
London W1M 5AP
☎ (020) 7486 8077

In the USA
Spanish National Tourist Office
666 Fifth Avenue, 35th floor
New York, NY 10103
☎ (212) 265-8822

Other SNTOs in Chicago, Los Angeles, Miami.

POLICE 091 Also for FIRE & AMBULANCE

FIRE In South: 080; in North: 922 32 81 80

AMBULANCE In South: 922 79 10 00; in North: 922 36 21 03

WHEN YOU ARE THERE

ARRIVING

By Air Almost all flights to Tenerife arrive at Reina Sofía (or Tenerife Sur) airport (☎ 922 75 90 00), on the Costa del Silencio near Playa de las Américas in the south of the island. A second airport, Los Rodeos (or Tenerife Norte, ☎ 922 63 58 00), at La Laguna in the north of the island, is used for some inter-island flights, some scheduled flights and some charters from Germany. Flights to La Gomera use a new airport at Playa de Santiago in the south of the island.
By Sea It is possible for independent travel-lers to reach the islands on a slow boat from Cadiz, on the Spanish mainland. The journey takes around two days. Inter-island ferries and hydrofoils connect Tenerife and La Gomera to the other islands.

Reina Sofía Airport to:	Journey times
Puerto de la Cruz: 100km	 2 hours
Playa de las Américas: 15km	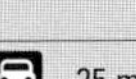 25 minutes

MONEY

Tenerife and La Gomera use the Spanish peseta (pta). Banknotes come in denominations of 1,000, 2,000, 5,000 and 10,000 ptas. As well as the one peseta coin, which has almost negligible value, coins are valued at 5, 10, 25, 50, 100, 200 and 500 ptas.
Prices may also be marked in Euros, which will replace pesetas altogether in 2002.

TIME

The time in Tenerife (and all the Canaries) is the same as in the UK, except where the annual change to and from Daylight Saving (or 'Summer Time') causes a temporary 1-hour time difference. The Canary Islands are 5 hours ahead of the eastern USA.

CUSTOMS

YES

There are no restrictions at all on goods taken into Tenerife or other Canary Islands.
It would be pointless to take most goods into these islands in the expectation of saving money, however: almost everything is cheaper in the Canaries than it is at home. If you are carrying a large amount of money, it may be worth declaring it on arrival to avoid explanations on departure.

NO

There are a few obvious exceptions to the information above, notably illegal drugs, firearms, obscene material and unlicensed animals.

EMBASSIES AND CONSULATES

UK	USA	Germany	Canada
Santa Cruz	Santa Cruz	Santa Cruz	Madrid
☎ 922 28 68 63	☎ 922 28 69 50	☎ 922 28 48 12	☎ 91/431 43 00

WHEN YOU ARE THERE

TOURIST OFFICES

- **Head office**: Cabildo Insular de Tenerife, Consejería de Turismo, Patronato de Turismo, Avenida José Antonio, Edif. del Cabildo, Santa Cruz ☎ 922 60 58 00

- **Local offices**: *Adeje*: Pueblo Torviscas ☎ 922 75 06 33

  La Orotava: 1 Plaza General Franco ☎ 922 33 00 50

  Playa de las Américas: Playa de Troya, Avenida Litoral ☎ 922 79 76 68 Puerto de la Cruz: Plaza de la Iglesia ☎ 922 38 60 00

  Reina Sofía Airport: ☎ 922 77 30 67

  Santa Cruz: Plaza de España ☎ 922 60 55 92

  Santiago del Teide: Playa de la Arena ☎ 922 10 03 48

- **La Gomera tourist office**: Pozo de la Aguada, Calle del Medio, San Sebastián ☎ 922 14 01 47

- **Website address**: The Spanish Tourist Office is at www.tourspain.es/inicioi.htm

NATIONAL HOLIDAYS

J	F	M	A	M	J	J	A	S	O	N	D
2	1	(2)	(1)	2	1	1	1	2	1	1	3

1 January	Año Nuevo (New Year's Day)
6 January	Los Reyes (Epiphany)
2 February	La Candelaria (Candlemas)
19 March	San José (St Joseph's Day)
March/April	Pascua (Easter) Thu, Fri, Sun of Easter Week, and following Mon
1 May	Dia del Trabajo (Labour Day)
May/June	Corpus Christi
25 July	Santiago (St James' Day)
15 August	Asunción (Assumption)
12 October	Hispanidad (Columbus Day)
1 November	Todos los Santos (All Saints' Day)
6 December	Constitucion (Constitution Day)
8 December	Immaculada Concepción (Immaculate Conception)
25 December	Navidad (Christmas)

OPENING HOURS

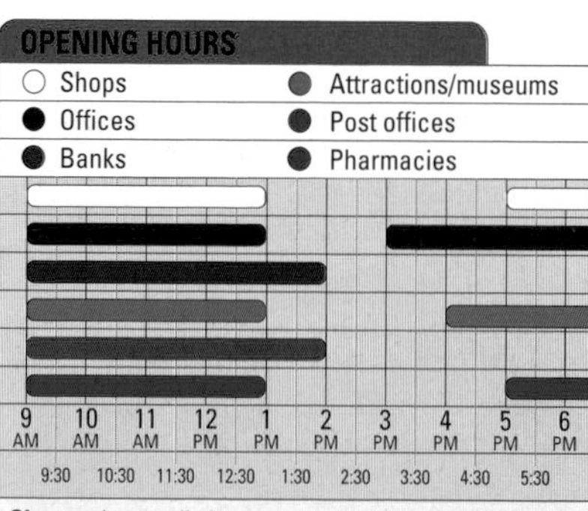

Shops: almost all shops are open Mon–Sat 9–1, 5–8.
Pharmacies: similar hours to shops but usually closed Sat afternoons. Normally at least one open after hrs.
Museums open 4–7PM, but some open mornings only.
Offices: usually Mon–Fri 9–1, 3–7.
Banks: Sat 9–1. (No Sat opening 1 Jun–31 Oct).
Post Offices: also open Sat 9–1.
Restaurants: lunch, noon–3PM; dinner 7PM – late.

PUBLIC TRANSPORT

Buses are always called by their local name, *guaguas* (pronounced wah-wahs). The stops are called *paradas* and are indicated by a letter P. A bus station is called an *Estación de Guaguas*. Most Tenerife buses are operated by TITSA, others by a smaller company called Transmersa (the two companies share a bus station in La Laguna). Services are fairly frequent and very inexpensive on main routes between towns. Off the main roads, and throughout La Gomera, service is intermittent and generally of little use to visitors.
If you plan to use buses a lot, save 25 per cent by purchasing a multi-trip TITSA-bono ticket.
Main bus stations: Playa de las Américas: Avenida Béthencourt ☎ 922 79 54 27
Santa Cruz: Avenida 3 Mayo ☎ 922 79 54 27
Puerto de la Cruz: Calle de Cupido ☎ 922 38 18 07
La Laguna: ☎ 922 25 94 12
Many of the main attractions operate shuttle buses to and from the resorts.

Ferries Transmediterránea (59 Calle La Marina, Santa Cruz ☎ 922 27 73 00): ferries to mainland Spain and other Canary Islands from Santa Cruz, car and passenger ferries from Los Cristianos to La Gomera.
Estación Jet-Foil (Muelle Norte, Santa Cruz ☎ 922 24 30 12): 80-minute jetfoil to Las Palmas de Gran Canaria.
Estación Hidro-Foil (Los Cristianos harbour ☎ 922 79 61 78): hydrofoils to La Gomera (35 mins).
Ferry Gomera (Los Cristianos harbour ☎ 922 79 05 56): car and passenger ferries to La Gomera (90 mins).
Fred Olsen (Ticket office, Muelle Ribera, Santa Cruz ☎ 922 62 82 00): to La Gomera and Gran Canaria several times a day from Santa Cruz.

CAR RENTAL

It is relatively inexpensive to hire a car on Tenerife, but pricier on La Gomera. The small local car firms are efficient (ask for an after-hours emergency number), though the more expensive international firms are also represented here. Drivers must be over 23.

TAXIS

Cabs display a special SP licence plate (*servicio público*). Some taxi ranks display fares between principal destinations. In addition, taxi drivers offer island tours for up to four passengers; call the Union of Taxi Workers on ☎ 922 21 00 59.

DRIVING

Speed limit on motorways: **100–120kph**

Speed limit on other main roads: **90kph**

Speed limit in towns: **60kph**

Seat belts are compulsory for all passengers. Children under 10 (excluding babies in rear-facing baby seats) must ride in the back seats. If you need child seats, it is strongly advised to book ahead.

Drink-driving: No on-the-road breath test is currently used, but driving under the influence of alcohol is strictly illegal; the consequences of being involved in an accident could extend to a jail term.

Petrol: Unleaded petrol (*sin plomo*) is the norm. Petrol stations on main roads are usually open 24hrs and most take credit cards. Off main roads, they may be far apart, closed on Sun, and don't always take credit cards.

Hired cars and their drivers should all be insured by the hire company. In the event of a breakdown, call the car hire company's emergency number.
Fines: hefty on-the-spot fines are levied for not wearing seat belts, not stopping at a Stop sign or overtaking where forbidden.

PERSONAL SAFETY

Crime is not a problem in Tenerife or La Gomera, except in tourist areas, where uniformed police are always in evidence. The greatest risk is assault or theft by another tourist. Put all bags, clothes, etc. in the boot of your car. If staying in a villa or apartment, lock doors and windows before going out.

- Fire is a risk in hotels – locate the nearest fire exit to your room and ensure it is not blocked or locked.
- Do not leave possessions unattended on the beach or in cars.

Police assistance:
☎ **091 from any call box**

TELEPHONES

To call the operator, dial 003. To use a phone in a bar, simply pay the charge requested at the end of the call – the barman has a meter to check the cost . To use a public pay phone, you'll usually need *una tarjeta de telefóno*, a phone card – widely available from tobacconists and similar shops.

International Dialling Codes

First dial 00, wait for a change of tone, then dial the country code, for example:

UK:	**44**
Ireland:	**353**
USA:	**1**
Spain:	**Dial number only**

There are also useful phone offices marked *Telefónica Internacional* where you pay a clerk after the call.

POST

Postboxes are yellow, and often have a slot marked *Extranjeros* for mail to foreign countries. Letters and postcards to the UK: 70ptas (up to 20gms). Air letters and postcards to the US/Canada: 120ptas (up to 15gms). Letters within Spain: 35ptas. Buy stamps at tobacconists, souvenir shops or post offices (*Correos y Telegrafos*).

ELECTRICITY

The voltage is 220/240v.

Sockets take the standard European two-round-pin plugs. Bring an adaptor for any British or American appliances you wish to use with their usual plugs, and Americans should change the voltage setting on appliances, or bring a voltage transformer.

TIPS/GRATUITIES

Yes ✓ No ✕

Hotels & Restaurants	✕	Incl
Room service	✕	50–100pta
Cafe/bar (round up bill to nearest 100pta	✓	
Taxis	✓	10%
Porters	✓	50–100pta
Chambermaids	✓	50–100pta
Ushers/usherettes at shows & events	✓	25–50pta
Hairdressers (women's)	3	200–300pta
Cloakroom/washroom attendant	✓	10–25pta
Tour guide	✓	200–300pta

What to Photograph: El Teide is the constant, ever-changing, moody presence in many Tenerife views. The volcanic terrain in the National Park, either as landscapes or in close up, provides extraordinary images. Lush colourful exotic vegetation makes a startling backdrop for holiday snaps.
Light: Be aware of the intensity of the light – early morning or evening may produce better effects.
Film: Most popular brands of colour or transparency film of normal speeds are readily available – others may be harder to find. Developing is cheaper in the UK.

HEALTH

Insurance

It is essential to have good medical health cover in case of a medical emergency. Hospital doctors within the state scheme will accept Form E111 from UK residents for free emergency treatment, but the process of reimbursement is complicated and bureaucratic. You may need to give a photocopy of Form E111 to the doctor. To claim on medical insurance you may need to show that you did request treatment under the E111 scheme.

Dental Services

Emergency treatment may be expensive but is covered by most medical insurance (but not by Form E111). Hotel receptionists and holiday reps can generally advise on a local dentist.

Sun Advice

The biggest danger to health here is too much sun. Remember that the Canaries are 700 miles nearer the Equator than southern Spain – on the same latitude as the Sahara. Use generous amounts of sun cream with a high protection factor. A wide-brimmed hat and a T-shirt (even when swimming) are advisable for children.

Medication

Any essential prescribed medications should be taken with you to Tenerife or La Gomera. The well-known over-the-counter proprietary brands of analgesics and popular remedies are available at all pharmacies. All medicines must be paid for, even if prescribed by a doctor.

Safe Water

Tap water is safe all over the islands, except where signs indicate that water is not drinkable. The taste may be slightly salty.

HOSPITALS AND CLINICS

Hotels can generally access medical assistance quickly in an emergency.
Santa Cruz Hospital General de Tenerife, Santa Cruz ☎ 922 65 21 52
Hospital Nuestra Señor de Candelaria, Santa Cruz. ☎ 922 53 17 99
Puerto de la Cruz and the North 24-hour English-speaking doctors: ☎ 900 100 090 (free call)
Medical Centre: ☎ 900 100 090 (free call)
Playa de las Américas and the South Centros Medicos del Sur Carretera Gen. del Sur, Playa de las Américas: 24-hour English-speaking doctors ☎ 922 79 10 00

CLOTHING SIZES

Tenerife	UK	Rest of Europe	USA	
46	36	46	36	Suits
48	38	48	38	
50	40	50	40	
52	42	52	42	
54	44	54	44	
56	46	56	46	
41	7	41	8	Shoes
42	7.5	42	8.5	
43	8.5	43	9.5	
44	9.5	44	10.5	
45	10.5	45	11.5	
46	11	46	12	
37	14.5	37	14.5	Shirts
38	15	38	15	
39/40	15.5	39/40	15.5	
41	16	41	16	
42	16.5	42	16.5	
43	17	43	17	
34	8	34	6	Dresses
36	10	36	8	
38	12	38	10	
40	14	40	12	
42	16	42	14	
44	18	44	16	
38	4.5	38	6	Shoes
38	5	38	6.5	
39	5.5	39	7	
39	6	39	7.5	
40	6.5	40	8	
41	7	41	8.5	

WHEN DEPARTING

- Always reconfirm your return flight with the airline or holiday rep at least one day before departing.
- Check in at least 90 minutes before flight departure.
- Allow time to return your hire car.

LANGUAGE

People working in the tourist industry, including waiters, generally know some English. In places where few tourists venture, including bars and restaurants in Santa Cruz, it is helpful to know some basic Spanish.

Pronunciation guide: *b* almost like a *v*; *c* before *e* or *i* sounds like *th* otherwise like *k*; *d* can be like English *d* or like a *th*; *g* before *e* or *i* is a guttural *h*, between vowels like *h*, otherwise like *g*; *h* always silent; *j* guttural *h*; *ll* like English *lli* (as in 'million'); *ñ* sounds like *ni* in 'onion'; *qu* sound like *k*; *v* sounds a little like *b*; *z* like English *th*.

hotel	*hotel*	breakfast	*el desayuno*
room	*una habitación*	bathroom	*el cuarto de baño*
single/double/twin	*individual/doble/con dos camas*	shower	*la ducha*
		balcony	*el balcón*
one/two nights	*una noche / dos noches*	reception	*la recepción*
		key	*la llave*
reservation	*una reserva*	room service	*el servicio de habitaciones*
rate	*la tarifa*		

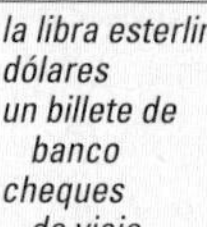

bureau de change	*cambio*	pounds sterling	*la libra esterlina*
post office	*correos*	US dollars	*dólares*
cash machine/ATM	*cajero automático*	banknote	*un billete de banco*
foreign exchange	*cambio (de divisas)*	travellers' cheques	*cheques de viaje*
foreign currency	*cambio*	credit card	*la tarjeta de crédito*

restaurant	*restaurante*	cheers!	*salud!*
cafe-bar	*bar*	dessert	*el postre*
table	*una mesa*	water	*agua*
menu	*la carta*	(house) wine	*vino (de la casa)*
set menus	*platos combinados*	beer	*cerveza*
		drink	*la bebida*
today's set menu	*el plato del día*	bill	*la cuentra*
wine list	*la carta de vinos*	the toilet	*los servicios*

plane	*el avion*	single/return...	*de ida / ...de ida y vuelta*
airport	*el aeropuerto*		
bus	*el autobús ('guagua')*	ticket office	*el despacho de billetes*
ferry	*el ferry*	timetable	*el horario*
terminal	*terminus*	seat	*un asiento*
ticket	*un billete*	reserved seat	*un asiento reservado*

yes	*si*	is there..?, do you have..?	*hay...?*
no	*no*		
please	*por favor*	I don't speak Spanish	*No hablo español*
thank you	*gracias*		
hello/hi	*hola!*	I am ...	*Soy ...*
hello/good day	*buenos dias*	I have ..	*Tengo ...*
sorry, pardon me	*perdon*	help!	*socorro!*
bye, see you	*hasta luego*	how much	*cuánto es?*
that's fine	*está bien*	open	*abierto*
what?	*como?*	closed	*cerrado*

INDEX

Author's Acknowledgements
The Automobile Association would like to thank the following photographers and libraries for their assistance in the preparation of this book.
MARY EVANS PICTURE LIBRARY 14b
INTERNATIONAL PHOTOBANK 6
MRI BANKERS' GUIDE TO FOREIGN CURRENCY 119
PICTURES COLOUR LIBRARY 90
PIRAMIDES DE GÜIMAR 44

The remaining photographs are held in the Association's own library (AA PHOTO LIBRARY) and were taken by: Rob Moore: Front Cover (c), 5b, 7b, 8c, 12c, 15a, 16a, 16b, 17a, 18a, 19, 20a, 20b, 21a, 22a, 23a, 24a, 25a, 25b, 26a, 37b, 38b, 40, 45, 49, 54b, 62b, 68, 72, 75a, 77b, 78b, 79b, 91a, 91b, 92, 93, 94, 95, 96, 97, 98, 99, 100, 101, 102, 103, 104, 105, 106, 107, 108, 109, 110, 111, 112, 113, 114, 115, 116; Clive Sawyer: Front Cover (a), Front Cover (b), 2, 9c, 10b, 12b, 17b, 18b, 21b, 22b, 23b, 26b, 31, 32a, 33a, 33b, 34a, 35a, 35b, 36, 37a, 38a, 39a, 42, 46, 47, 50a, 51a, 51b, 55b, 56a, 56b, 57b, 59b, 59c, 60/61, 63b, 69b, 70b, 70c, 74b, 75b, 80, 81, 82a, 82/83, 83a, 83b, 84, 85a, 85b, 86a, 86b, 87a, 87b, 88, 89a, 89b, 117a, 117b; J A Tims: Front Cover (d), Back Cover, 1, 5a, 6a, 7a, 8a, 8b, 9a, 9b, 9d, 10a, 11a, 11b, 12a, 13a, 13b, 14a, 15b, 24b, 27a, 27b, 28, 29, 30, 32b, 34b, 34c, 35c, 39b, 41, 43, 48, 50b, 52, 53, 54a, 55a, 57a, 58, 59a, 61, 62a, 63a, 64, 65a, 65b, 66, 67a, 67b, 69a, 70a, 71a, 71b, 71c, 73, 74a, 76, 77a, 78a, 79a, 122a, 122b, 122c.

Copy editor: Lynn Bresler

Dear Essential Traveller

Your comments, opinions and recommendations are very important to us. So please help us to improve our travel guides by taking a few minutes to complete this simple questionnaire.

You do not need a stamp (unless posted outside the UK). If you do not want to cut this page from your guide, then photocopy it or write your answers on a plain sheet of paper.

Send to: **The Editor, AA World Travel Guides, FREEPOST SCE 4598, Basingstoke RG21 4GY.**

Your recommendations...

We always encourage readers' recommendations for restaurants, nightlife or shopping – if your recommendation is used in the next edition of the guide, we will send you a ***FREE* AA *Essential* Guide** of your choice. Please state below the establishment name, location and your reasons for recommending it.

____

____

____

____

Please send me **AA *Essential*** _______________
(*see list of titles inside the front cover*)

About this guide...

Which title did you buy?
AA *Essential* _______________
Where did you buy it? _______________
When? m m / y y

Why did you choose an AA *Essential* Guide? _______________

____

____

____

____

Did this guide meet your expectations?
Exceeded ☐ Met all ☐ Met most ☐ Fell below ☐
Please give your reasons _______________

____

____

____

continued on next page...

Were there any aspects of this guide that you particularly liked? ______________

____

____

____

Is there anything we could have done better? ______________________

____

____

____

____

About you...

Name (*Mr/Mrs/Ms*) ______________________________

Address ______________________________________

____

______________________ Postcode ______________

Daytime tel nos ______________________________

Which age group are you in?

Under 25 ☐ 25–34 ☐ 35–44 ☐ 45–54 ☐ 55–64 ☐ 65+ ☐

How many trips do you make a year?

Less than one ☐ One ☐ Two ☐ Three or more ☐

Are you an AA member? Yes ☐ No ☐

About your trip...

When did you book? m m / y y When did you travel? m m / y y

How long did you stay? ______________________________

Was it for business or leisure? ______________________

Did you buy any other travel guides for your trip?

If yes, which ones? ______________________________

____

Thank you for taking the time to complete this questionnaire. Please send it to us as soon as possible, and remember, you do not need a stamp (*unless posted outside the UK*).

Happy Holidays!

The AA and the Automobile Association Limited, their subsidiaries and any other companies or bodies in which either has an interest ('the AA Group') may use information about you to provide you with details of other products and services, by telephone or in writing. The AA Group as a matter of policy does not release its lists to third parties.
If you do not wish to receive further information please tick the box... ☐